Easy Christmas Favorites for Tin Whistle or Irish Flute

by Grey Larsen

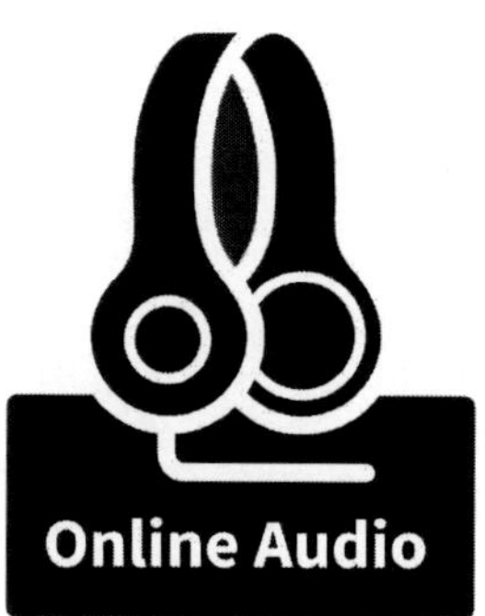

To access online audio recordings go to:

WWW.MELBAY.COM/30788MEB

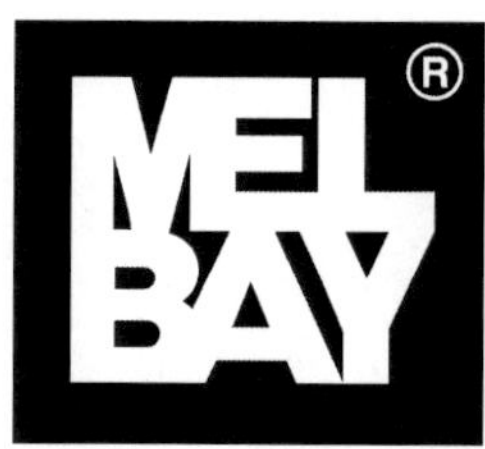

WWW.MELBAY.COM

Table of Contents

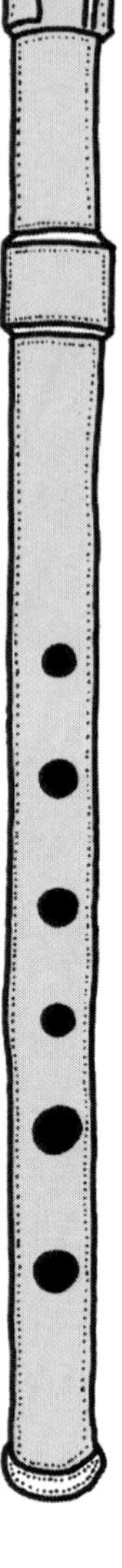

Credits
Illustrations: Sam Bartlett
Back Cover Photo: Shannon Zahnle
Audio Production: Grey Larsen Mastering

Audio Recordings
Grey Larsen: tin whistle and Irish flute
Cindy Kallet: guitar
Tin whistle used: Session D from Carbony Celtic Winds
Irish Flute used: Firth, Pond & Co., 1848-1863, with headjoint by Chris Abell, 2007
Guitar used: Michael Gurian, c. 1970

I offer my heartfelt thanks to Cindy Kallet for her editorial assistance, and for her beautiful guitar playing.

Introduction

Welcome! I hope you'll enjoy this collection of 30 Christmas carols and songs arranged for tin whistle or Irish flute. (Tin whistles are also known as pennywhistles.)

These pieces originated in Europe and the United States. A number of them have roots going back to medieval times, and some are descended from early instrumental dance tunes.

This book provides whistle and flute players with easy-to-play arrangements of these holiday favorites. The songs translate beautifully to the whistle and flute because wind players breathe and phrase much the way singers do.

What Makes These Tunes Easy?

- They are played in the lower two octaves of the whistle and flute's range, ascending no higher than B in the second octave. (Notes above this can be challenging to play on the whistle, and they sound too loud and shrill to many people.)
- They are in easy whistle and flute keys or modes: D major, G major, E minor, B minor and A Dorian.
- They use only the eight **primary notes** of the D whistle and Irish flute. Using the widely accepted symbol for "sharp" (♯), and progressing from the lowest note upward, step by step, these notes are:

D, E, F♯, G, A, B, C and C♯

There are four *non-primary* notes as well — E-flat (E♭), F-natural (F♮), G-sharp (G♯) and B-flat (B♭) — but they are not easily played on the D whistle or keyless Irish flute as they require techniques called "half-holing" or "cross-fingering." The tunes in this book don't use those notes.

Which Whistle or Flute Should You Use With This Book?

The tin whistle in D is widely considered to be the standard one, and I recommend using it with this book. You can also use the standard Irish flute. It's in D as well, and uses the exact same fingerings as the D whistle. You can also play these tunes on the modern, Boehm-system flute and piccolo, as well as soprano and tenor recorders.

The D whistle comes in two forms: the **small D**, which measures about 12 inches in length (or about 29 centimeters), and the **low D**, which is twice as long and plays one octave lower. You can use either one, though the low D is more challenging to play. You'll hear a small D whistle used on the online recordings for this book.

You can also use a non-D whistle. Whistles that are longer and lower than the small D have mellower voices and can be very satisfying to play. If your hands are very small, however, or compromised in some way, and you find it difficult to manage the small D whistle, you might want to use one that is shorter, such as a whistle in E-flat (E♭), E, F, F-sharp (F♯) or G.

When using a non-D whistle and reading the tunes in this book, pretend you are fingering the notes on a D whistle. You may want to refer to the fingering chart for D whistle and Irish flute on p. 5. If you use a whistle that is pitched lower than the small D, the tunes will sound lower than written. If you use one that plays higher than the small D, the tunes will sound higher than written.

To play along with the audio files using a non-D whistle, you'll want to use a device or software application to raise or lower the pitch of these files to match the pitch level of the whistle you're playing.

Audio Recordings Included

At www.melbay.com/30788MEB you can access audio recordings in which I play all 30 songs on a small D whistle and on Irish flute.

Chords are included with the notation and recording of each tune. On the recordings the chords are played on guitar, but they can be played on other instruments as well. Recordings of each tune are provided in several configurations: whistle alone, Irish flute alone, guitar alone, whistle with guitar, and Irish flute with guitar.

If You Need Help With Tin Whistle or Irish Flute Playing

If you are new to the tin whistle, have questions about it or need help with your playing, I recommend you consult my book *First Lessons Tin Whistle*. It offers valuable insights as well as thorough instruction for beginners. If you are new to the Irish flute, I recommend working with my book *The Essential Guide to Irish Flute and Tin Whistle*.

Two Forms of Notation

This book uses standard music notation. If you don't read music I encourage you to learn how, as it is a rich and useful notation system. There are many books and online resources that explain how it works.

However, if you don't read music, don't worry — you can still make good use of this book, as each tune is also notated in tin whistle and Irish flute **tablature**. Tablature is an instrument-specific system that graphically illustrates a fingering for each note. Tablature systems exist for many instruments and have been in use at least since the 1300s. Below I explain how tin whistle and Irish flute tablature works. (This tablature system does not work for the modern Boehm-system flute and piccolo, or for soprano and tenor recorders, because their fingerings differ from those of the Irish flute and tin whistle.)

Tin Whistle and Irish Flute Tablature

This form of tin whistle and Irish flute tablature uses a **staff** — a set of parallel horizontal lines. You may encounter others which do not, such as those that use a picture of a whistle for each note.

Have a look at the tablature, below, for the beginning of "The First Noel." The tablature staff appears above the music notation staff.

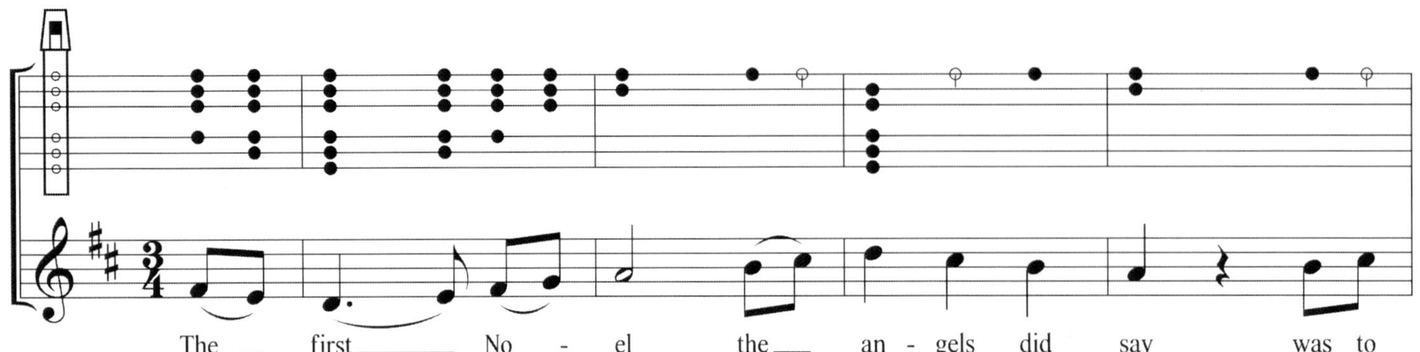

This tablature system features five elements:

1. A tin whistle icon, or **clef**, at the left edge of the tablature staff. Its six small circles represent the six finger holes of the whistle or Irish flute. The presence of this clef identifies the staff as a whistle or Irish flute tablature staff.

2. Six horizontal, parallel staff lines extending through and to the right of the clef. Notice that each staff line goes through a finger hole circle on the clef. Each staff line therefore represents one of the six finger holes of the whistle or Irish flute. The top group of three staff lines corresponds to the top-hand finger holes while the bottom group of three lines corresponds to the bottom-hand finger holes.

3. Solid black dots. For each note (with the exception of C♯) you'll see one or more solid black circles, or dots, centered upon the staff lines and vertically aligned with each other. (These dots are never placed between, above or below the staff lines.) Each dot indicates a closed finger hole. For example, the tune's sixth note, low G, has dots upon each of the top three staff lines. This shows that you finger low G by closing the top three finger holes and leaving the bottom three holes open.

4. A special fingering symbol — ⚲ — for the note C♯. Since we finger C♯ by opening all six finger holes, I use this special symbol for that note, and that note only. You can see this symbol above, in measures 3, 4 and 5. Its open circle indicates an open finger hole, while its small descending line suggests that open holes extend all the way down the whistle.

5. Barlines. These are vertical lines that cut through the six-line staff and divide the music, as it flows from left to right, into time segments which are typically of equal duration. These segments of time are referred to as **measures** or **bars**. (The pickup measure that begins this tune, however, is a partial measure; it has fewer beats than do the other measures, even though they all share the same time signature.)

Tablature does not tell you much about the rhythm of the music. If you don't read music and are unfamiliar with the rhythms of a tune, you'll need to learn those rhythms by listening to its recording.

A Fingering Chart for the D Tin Whistle and Irish Flute

The following chart shows the primary notes of the D whistle and Irish flute, along with their fingerings. (Note that the small D whistle sounds one octave higher than written.) Uppercase letters indicate low-register notes, while lowercase letters indicate high-register notes. This manner of using upper and lowercase letters is also a feature of *abc notation*, a music notation system widely used on the internet at the time of this writing.

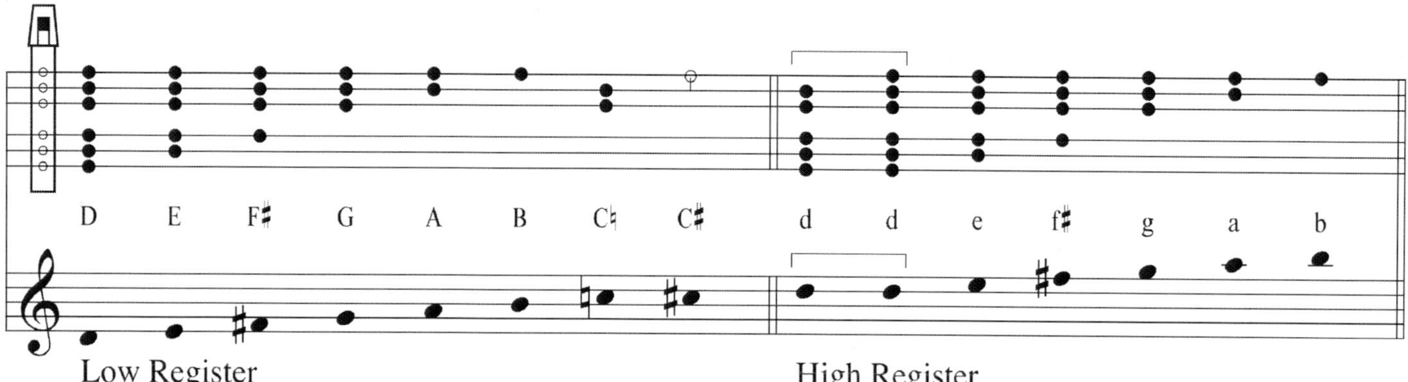

This chart shows two fingerings for high D, joined under a bracket. I use only the first of these fingerings in the tablature throughout this book. (It's often called the "vented" D fingering, because the top hole is open, or vented.) I generally prefer this fingering for its clarity of tone and because you cannot play low D by mistake when using it. However, you may sometimes want to use the other fingering (which is the same as the fingering for low D) to reduce the number and complexity of your finger movements. (There is more information on these high D fingering options in *First Lessons Tin Whistle*.)

Lyrics

Lyrics are provided for the initial verse of each song, and for the refrain when there is one. For many of these songs there are multiple variants or versions of the lyrics, and it's often hard to know which one, if any, to consider definitive. To find other versions, as well as the lyrics to subsequent verses, you can search online or consult other sources.

Slurs and Phrasing

The slurs you see in the following pages conform to the way the lyrics underlay the melodies. As a whistle or flute player, you need not be bound by such lyric-based phrasing. Use slurring, tonguing and phrasing in any way that appeals to you. On the recordings you'll hear me do just that. I also use vibrato from time to time.

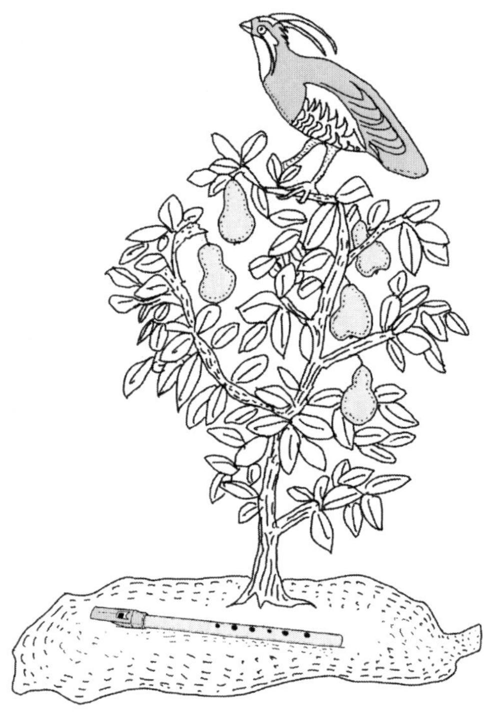

Breathing

You'll find rests in all the tunes. They provide excellent breathing places. However, you'll need more places to breathe than those supplied by the rests. Create additional breathing places by shortening notes as needed. You'll hear me do this on the recordings.

More About the Chords

Some of these carols have been around for centuries, and musicians have devised many ways to harmonize and accompany them. My guitar accompanist and I have crafted chordal arrangements that appeal to us; feel free to change them to suit your musical taste. You may be playing a different accompaniment instrument, such as a keyboard, which has idiomatic capabilities that differ from those of the guitar.

The chords in the following pages are shown in root position (i.e., the root of the chord is its lowest note). However, on the recordings you'll hear the guitar occasionally play the third or fifth of the chord as the lowest note. This helps to create pleasing bass lines when moving from chord to chord. Feel free to use bass notes that appeal to you.

Also, if you're playing a fretted string instrument, such as a guitar, you may at times want to use a capo to simplify your chord fingerings.

Playing the Tunes in Other Keys

24 of these pieces can be played in two different keys (for example, D major and G major), using just the primary notes of the whistle and Irish flute. One of them, "In the Bleak Midwinter," can be played in three keys (in D, G and A major). In this book each melody is presented in only one key, but you can download versions notated in other keys (along with corresponding audio files) at greylarsen.com/xef.

Whistle or Flute Duets

It's great fun to play these tunes with another whistle or flute player when one of you plays a harmony part. In this book I provide three such duets, which you'll find on pp. 40—45. You might also enjoy playing the harmony part when the song is being sung.

With each duet, the melody part appears on the left-facing page and the harmony part on the right. Audio for these three duets is included in the downloads that come with this book, in several variants: each whistle or flute part alone, both whistle or flute parts together, and each of those with and without guitar accompaniment.

These duets can also work very well when played by other melodic instruments.

The duet harmony parts are designed to work with the chords that are shown. If you change the chords, be aware that the harmony part may need to be adjusted accordingly.

Another Book of Easy Tin Whistle or Irish Flute Tunes

You might enjoy *Easy Favorites for Tin Whistle or Irish Flute*, another book of easy tune arrangements, this one featuring a variety of folksongs and other well-loved melodies. Like this book, it comes with music notation, chords, tin whistle and Irish flute tablature, as well as audio files featuring tin whistle and Irish flute, with and without guitar, and guitar-only recordings to accompany you as you play the tunes.

For a list of my other Irish flute and tin whistle repertoire and instruction books, please see p. 46.

Further Online Resources

You'll find the following at greylarsen.com/xef:

- 25 of this book's 30 tunes notated in alternate keys, along with corresponding audio files
- Exercises for tin whistle and Irish flute finger coordination, with audio files
- Blank templates for notating your own tin whistle and Irish flute tablature
- Excerpts from my other books
- Links to tin whistle and Irish flute videos

Now, on to the tunes!

THE MUSIC

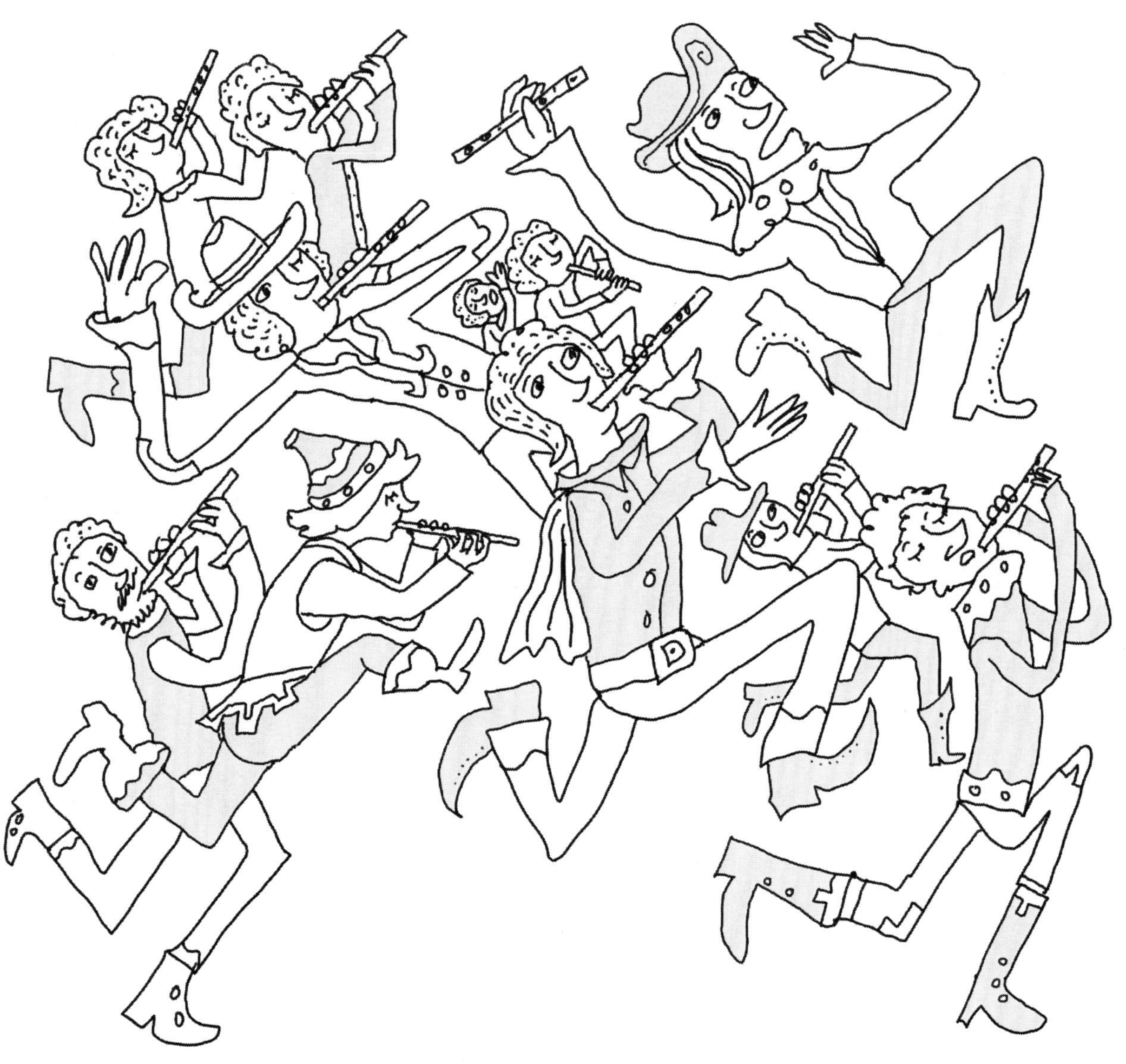

Angels We Have Heard on High

This melody is from an old French carol, "Les Anges dans nos compagnes." The English lyrics most often sung today were probably written in 1862 by James Chadwick, Bishop of Hexham and Newcastle, and were inspired by the words of the original French song.

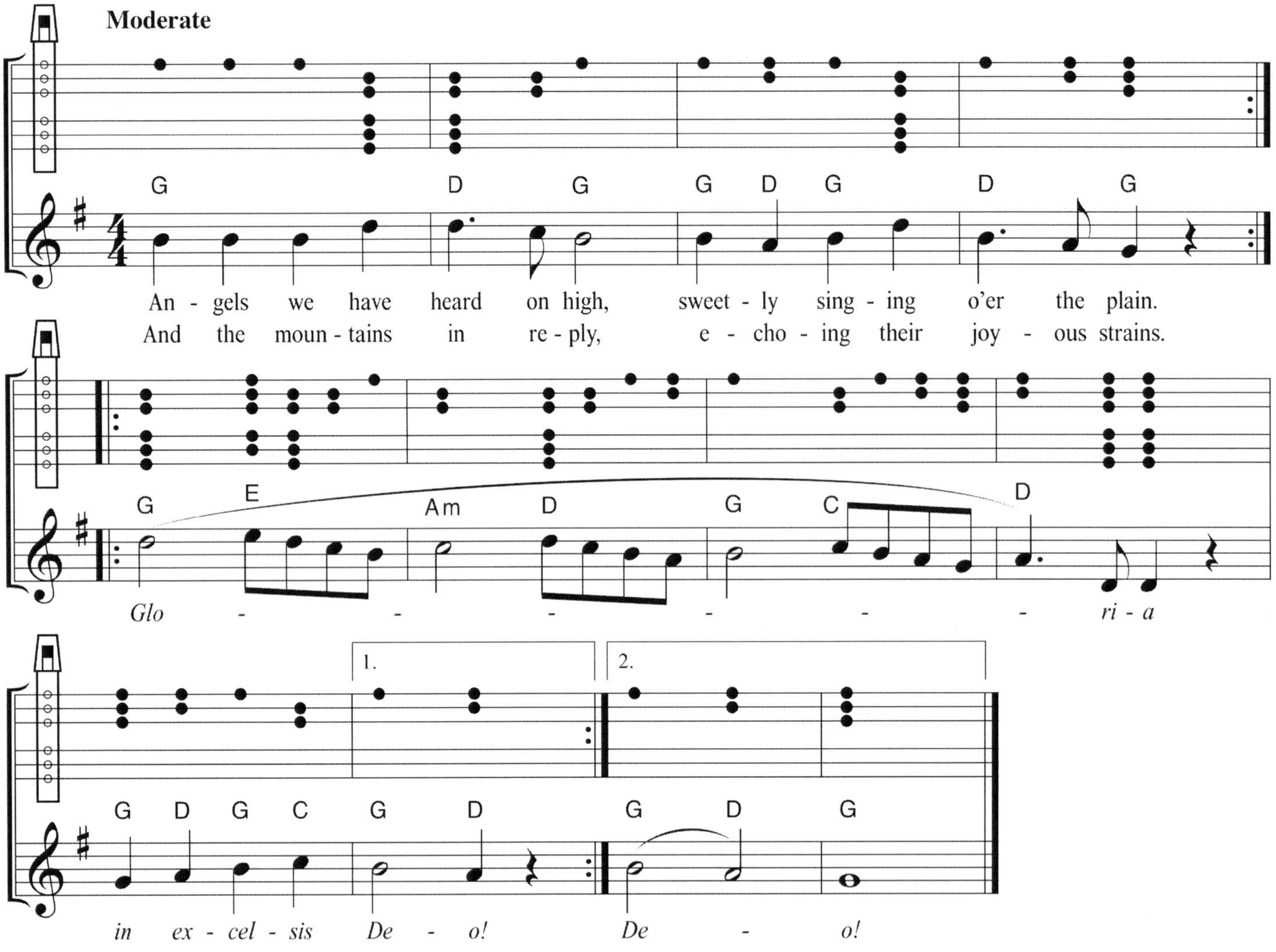

Moderate

G D G G D G D G

An - gels we have heard on high, sweet - ly sing - ing o'er the plain.
And the moun - tains in re - ply, e - cho - ing their joy - ous strains.

G E Am D G C D

Glo - - - - - - ri - a

1. 2.

G D G C G D G D G

in ex - cel - sis De - o! De - o!

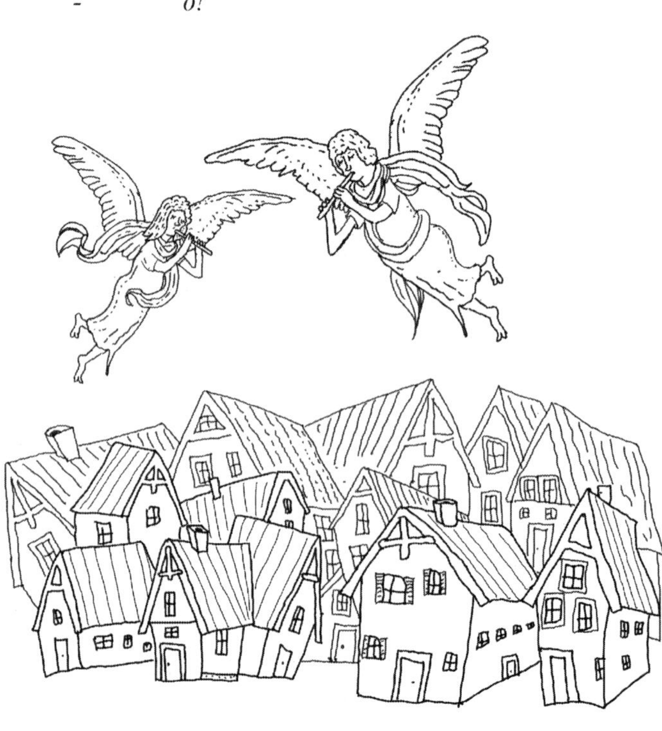

Away in a Manger

This carol was first published in the late 19th century and is now thought to be entirely American in origin. Some have claimed that Martin Luther wrote the first two verses, but there seems to be little evidence of this. The melody may be by James Ramsey Murray (1841—1905), the editor of the song's first publication in 1887.

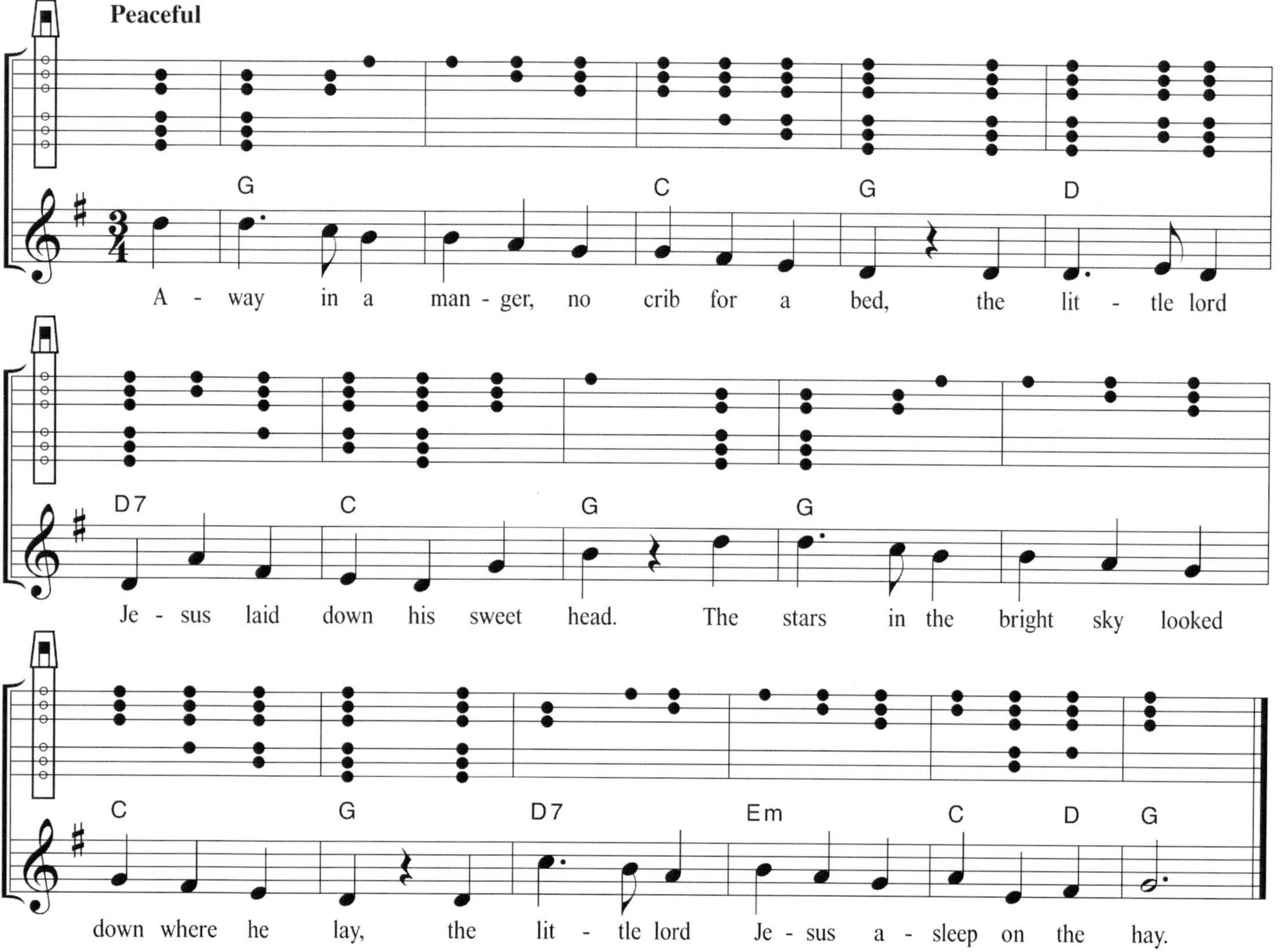

The Boar's Head Carol

This is a 15th century English carol depicting the ancient tradition of sacrificing a boar and presenting its head at a Yuletide feast. Its lyrics are in English and Latin. This setting of the carol is based on a version published in London in 1521 in Wynkyn de Worde's *Christmasse Carolles*.

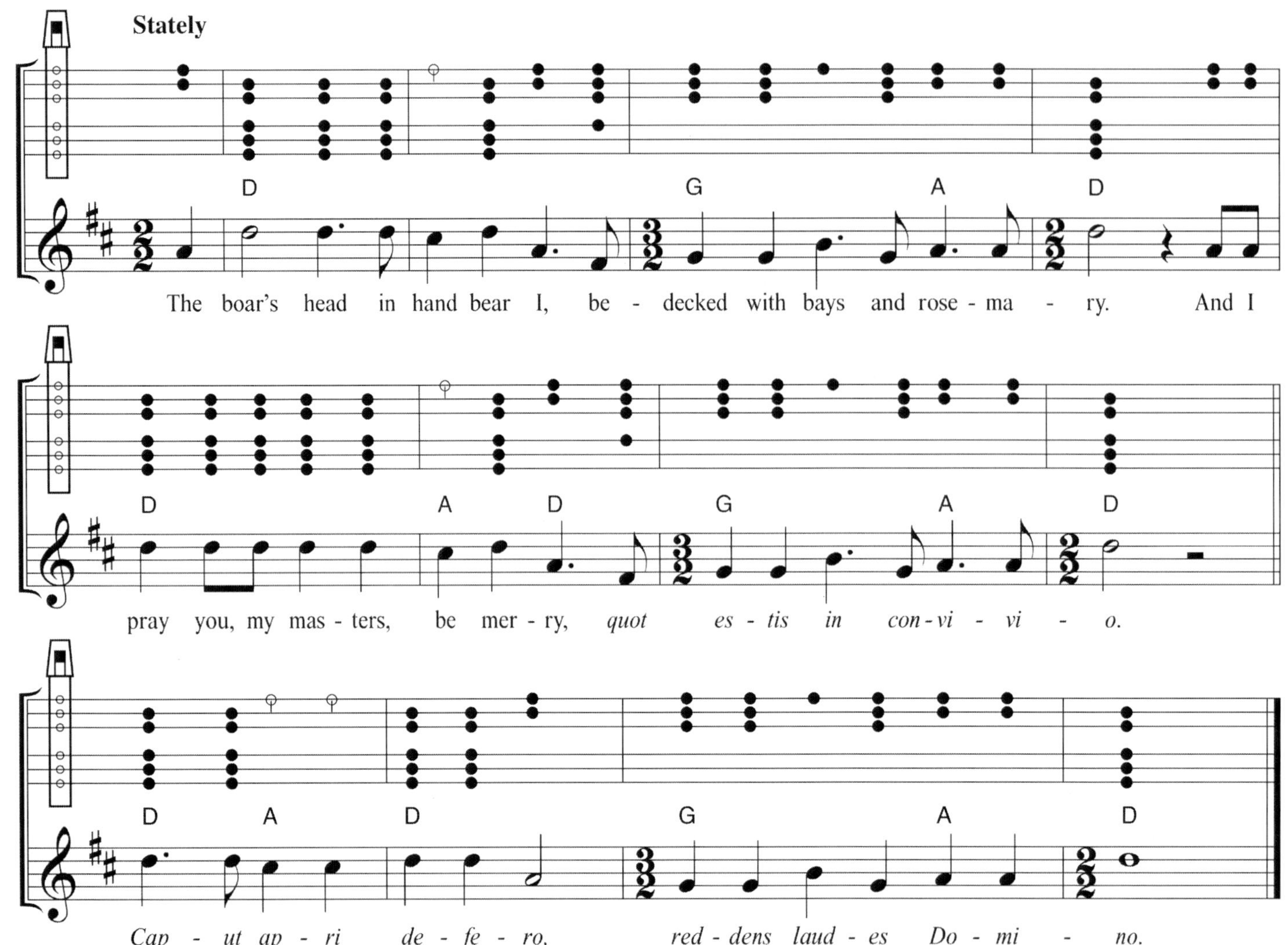

Bring a Torch, Jeanette, Isabella

This 17th century French carol "Un flambeau, Jeannette, Isabelle" came from the Provence region. The melody may be by Marc-Antoine Charpentier (1643—1704). On Christmas Eve in Provence, children dressed as shepherds and milkmaids, carrying torches and candles, sing this carol on their way to Midnight Mass.

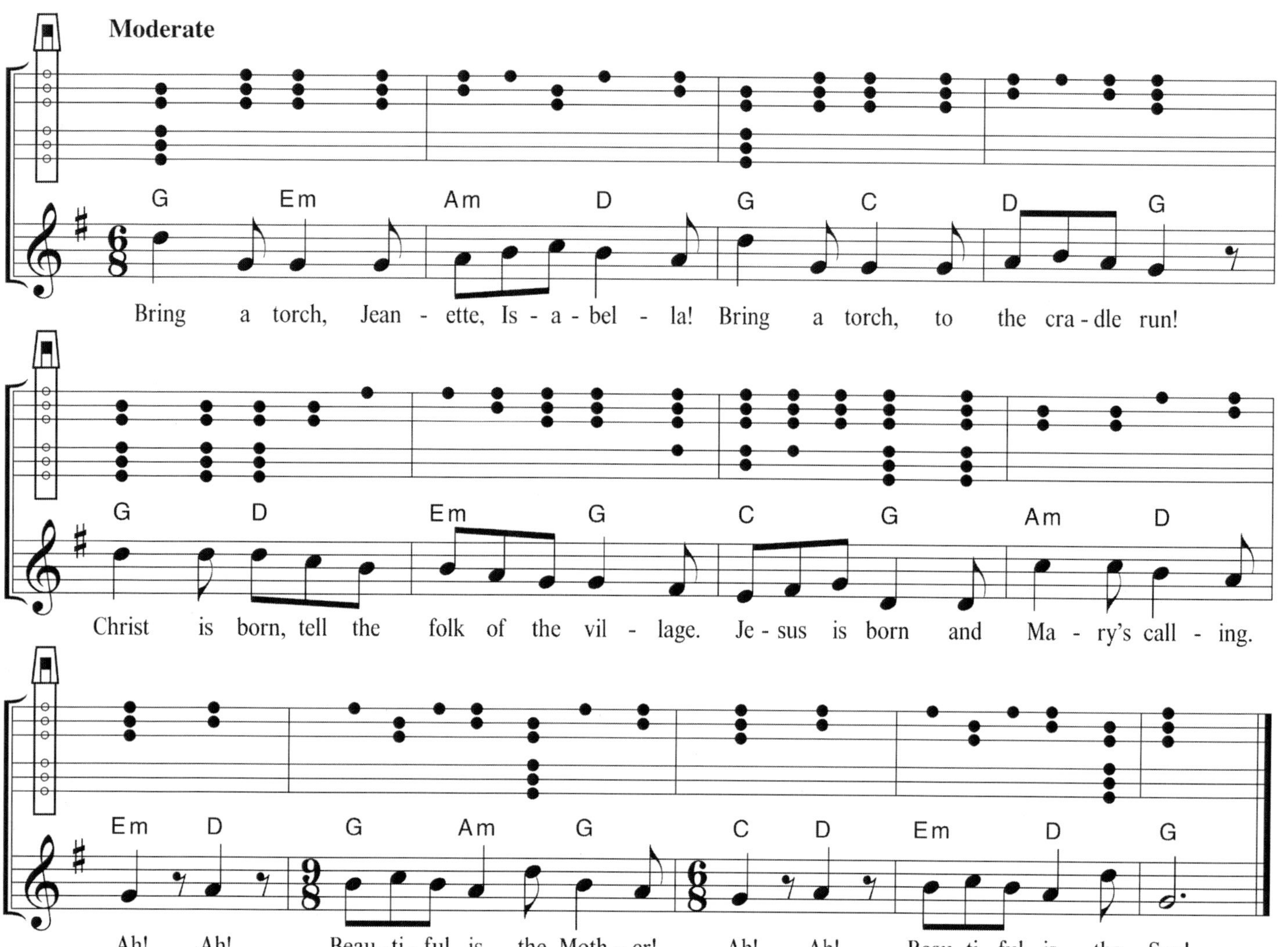

Deck the Halls

The melody of this Christmas and New Year's carol is from the Welsh winter carol "Nos Galan" (New Year's Eve) and dates to the 16th century. The English lyrics are thought to have been written by Scottish musician Thomas Oliphant in 1862. The repeated "fa la la" syllables may derive from medieval Welsh balladry.

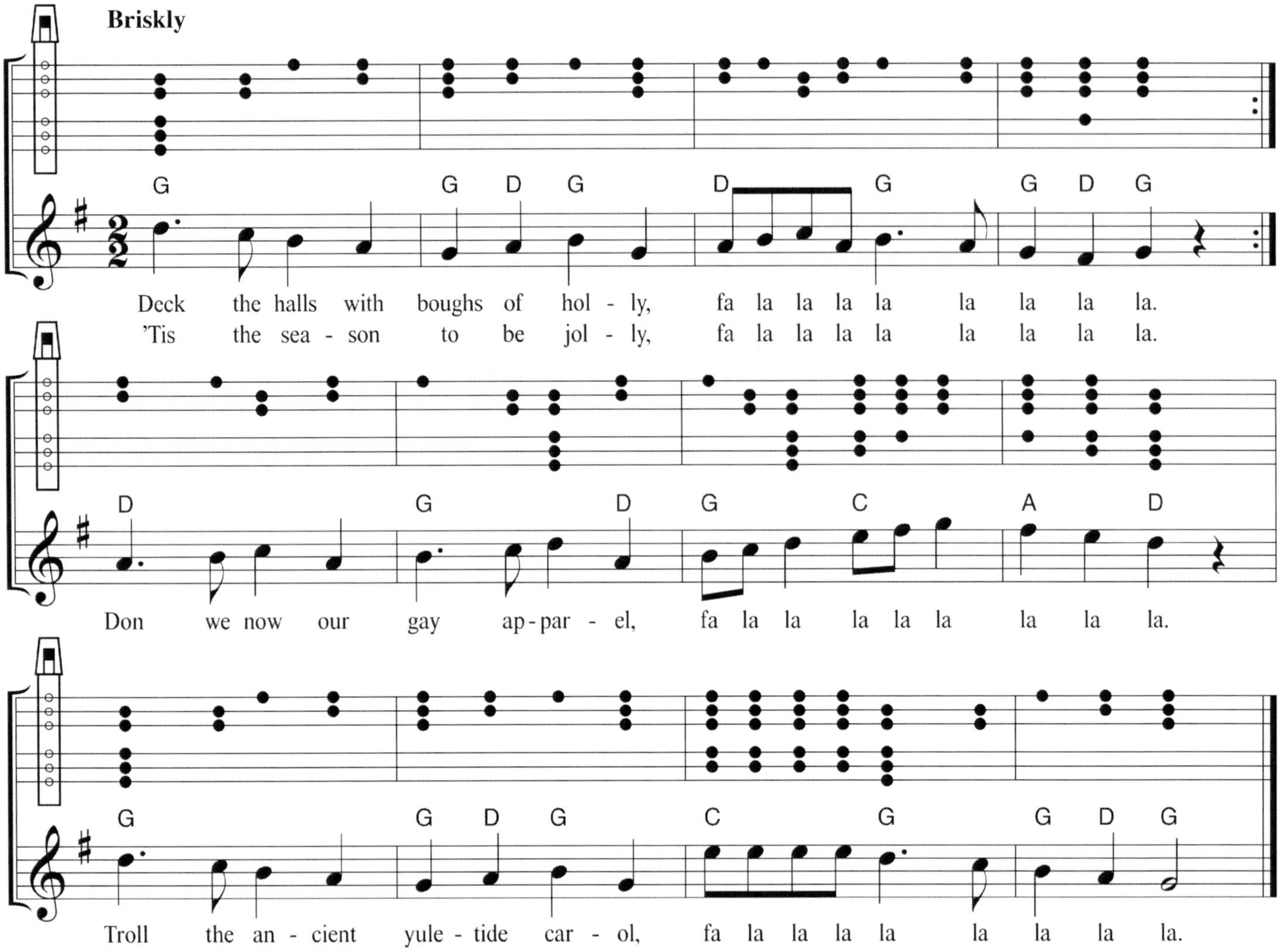

Briskly

G G D G D G G D G

Deck the halls with boughs of hol - ly, fa la la la la la la la la.
'Tis the sea - son to be jol - ly, fa la la la la la la la la.

D G D G C A D

Don we now our gay ap - par - el, fa la la la la la la la la.

G G D G C G G D G

Troll the an - cient yule - tide car - ol, fa la la la la la la la la.

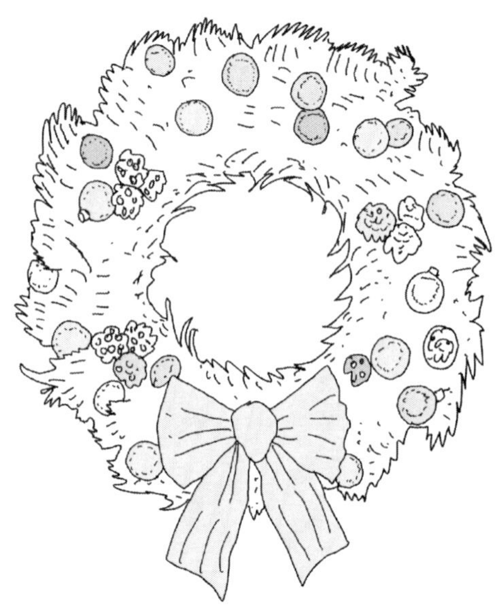

Ding Dong Merrily on High

The melody of this carol is a French folk dance tune which first appeared as "Branle de l'Official" in a dance treatise written by Jehan Tabourot (1519—1595). The English and Latin lyrics were written by English composer George Ratcliffe Woodward (1848—1934), who had a keen interest in church bell ringing.

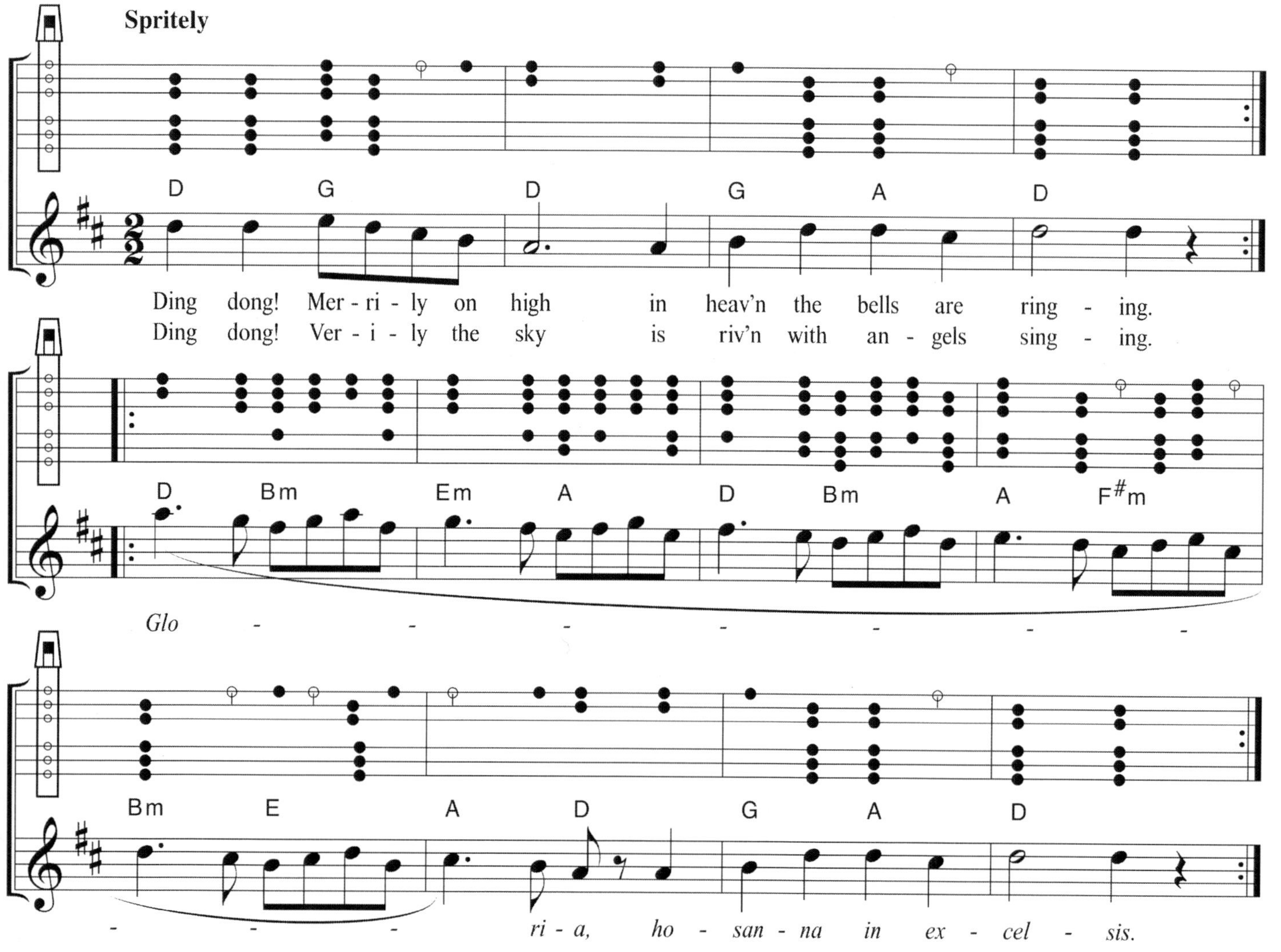

The First Noel

This carol may be from Cornwall and dates to the 1600s or earlier. It may have originally been sung more for Epiphany than for Christmas. It was first published in its current form in 1823. Today it is often sung in a four-part arrangement, first published in 1871, by the English composer John Stainer.

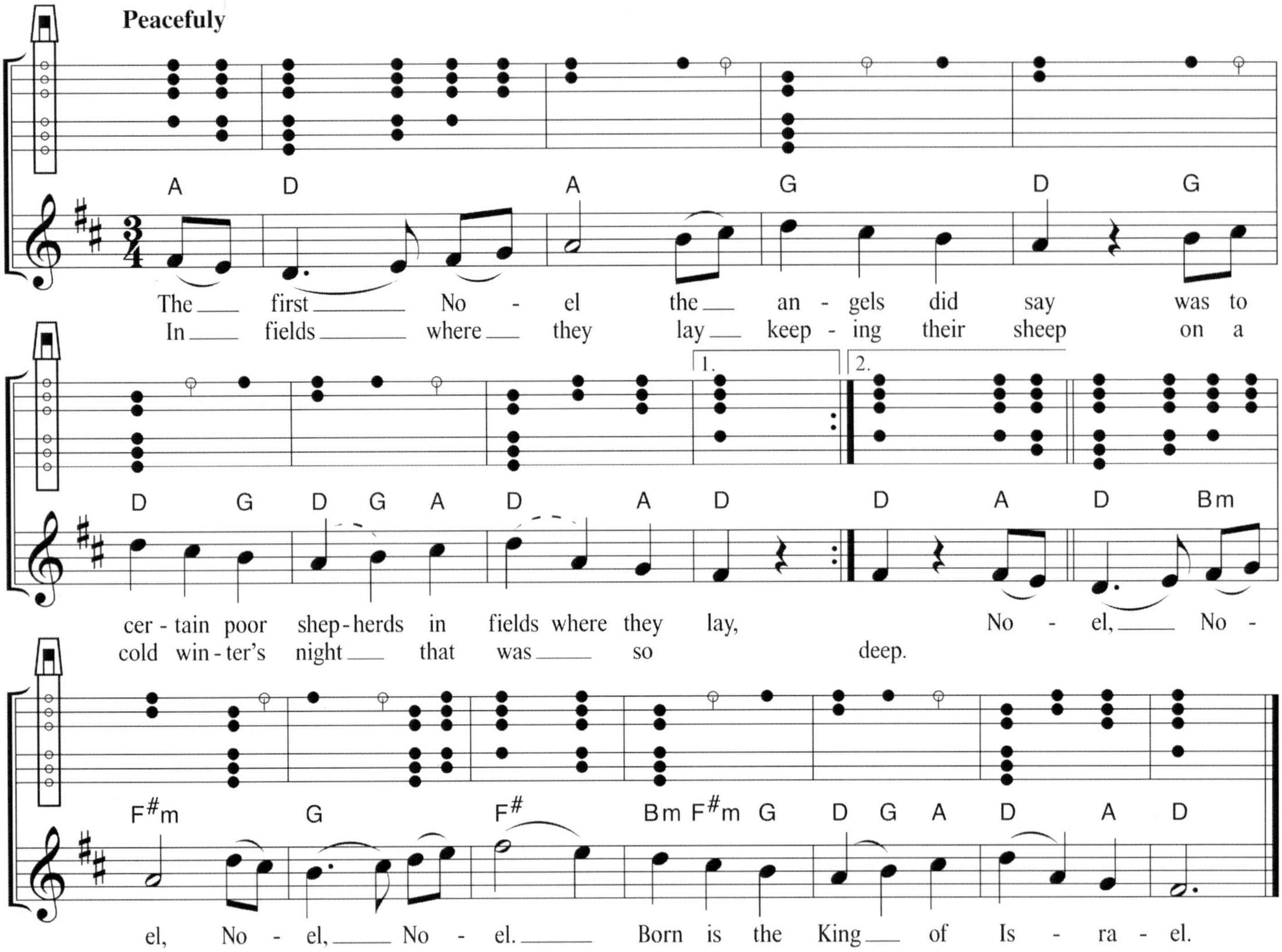

Peacefuly

A D A G D G

The first No - el the an - gels did say was to
In fields where they lay keep - ing their sheep on a

D G D G A D A D D A D Bm

cer - tain poor shep - herds in fields where they lay, No - el, No -
cold win - ter's night that was so deep.

F#m G F# Bm F#m G D G A D A D

el, No - el, No - el. Born is the King of Is - ra - el.

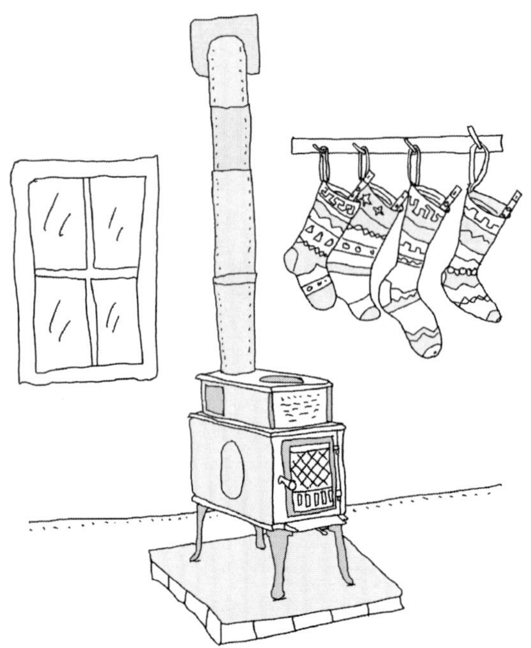

Go Tell It on the Mountain

This is a traditional African American spiritual and Christmas carol dating at least back to 1865. It was compiled into its present form by John Wesley Work, Jr. (1871—1925), a songwriter and collector of folksongs and spirituals. Work studied at Fisk and Harvard Universities and directed the Fisk Jubilee Singers.

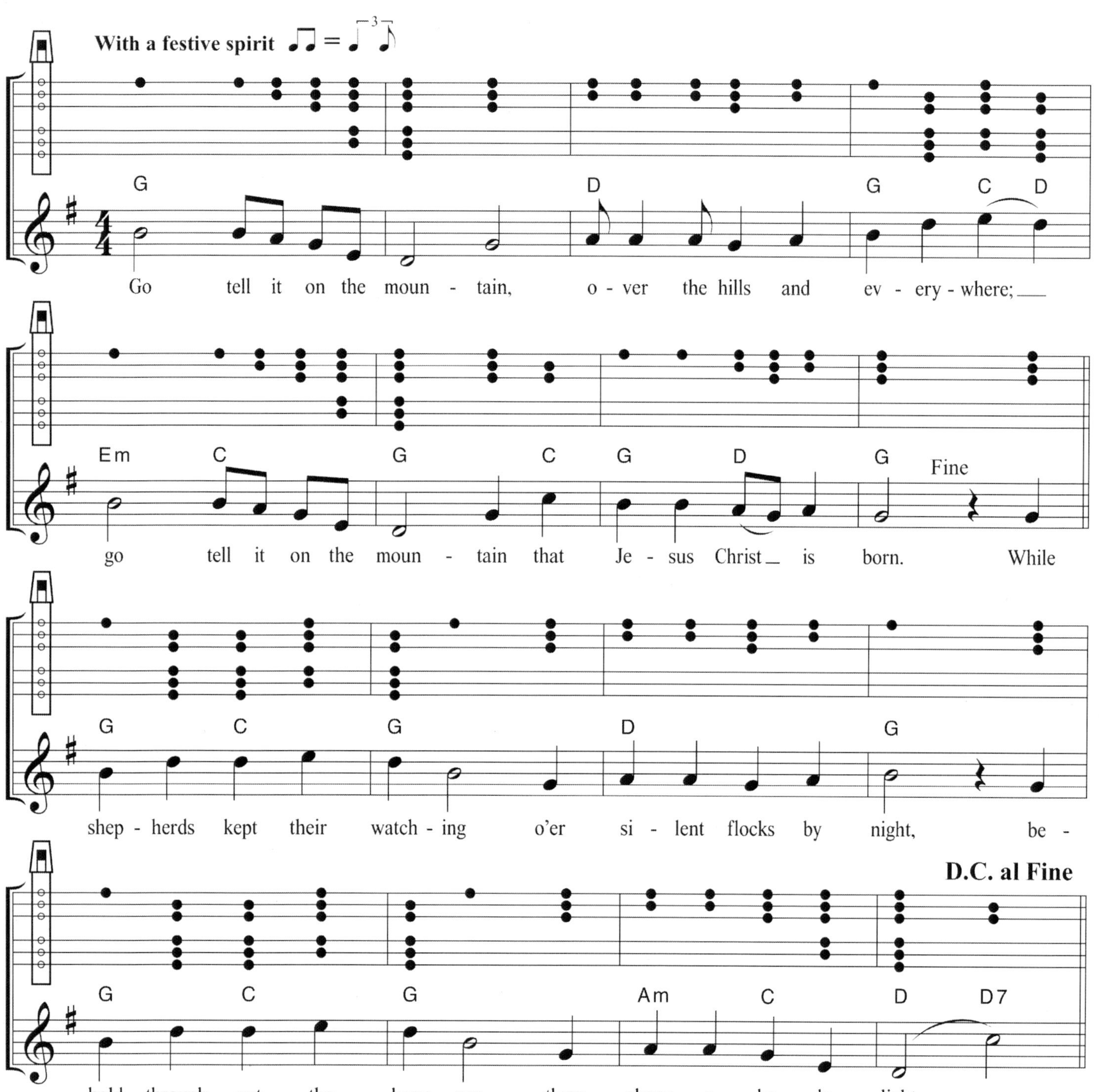

God Rest Ye Merry, Gentlemen

This English carol dates from the 16th century or earlier. The earliest known printed version is from a 1760 English broadside. Charles Dickens refers to this carol in his 1843 novella, *A Christmas Carol*: "… at the first sound of 'God bless you, merry gentlemen! May nothing you dismay!', Scrooge seized the ruler with such energy of action that the singer fled in terror, leaving the keyhole to the fog and even more congenial frost."

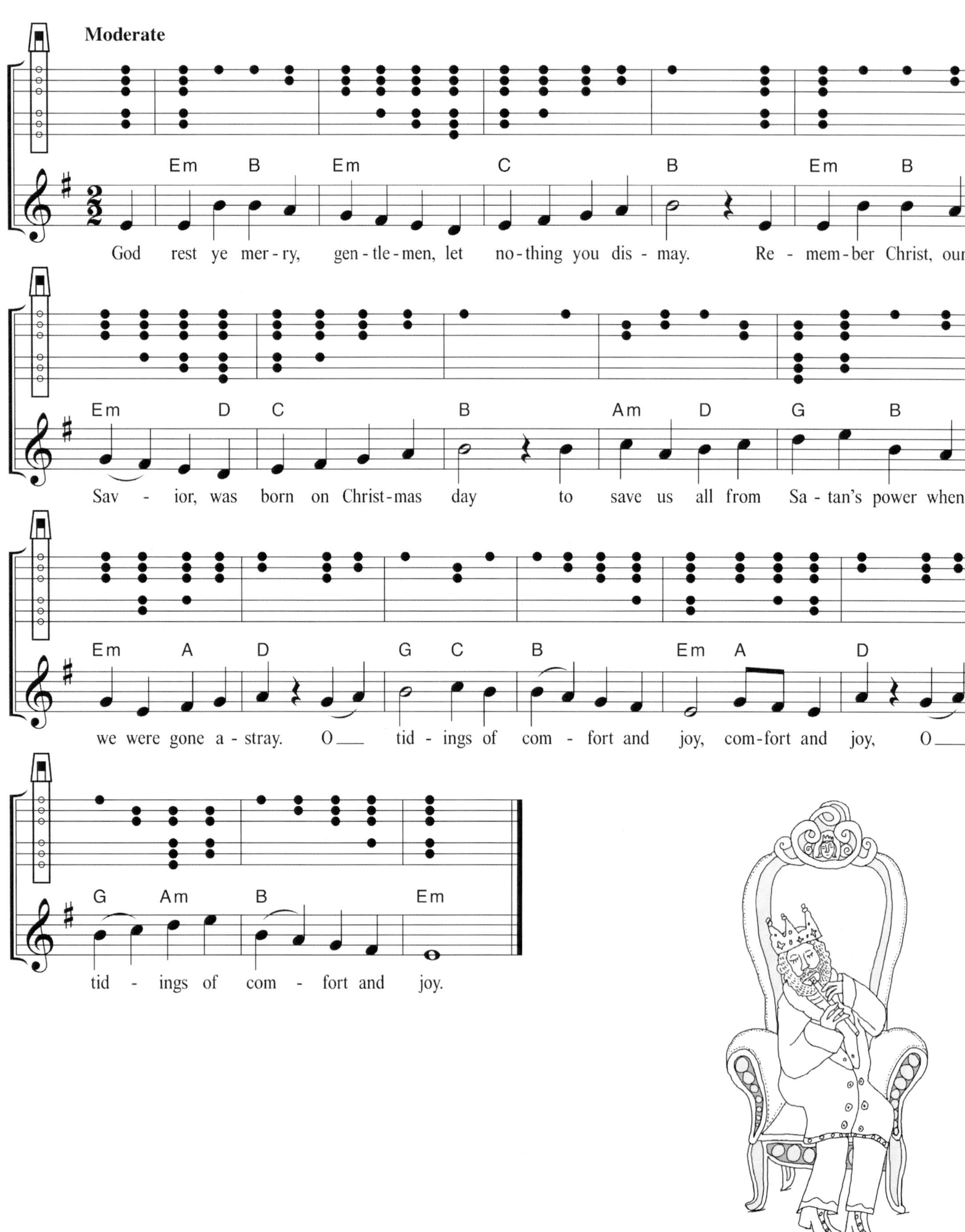

Good King Wenceslas

English hymn writer John Mason Neale (1818—1866) wrote this carol's lyrics in 1853, setting them to the 13th century spring carol "Tempus adest floridum," first published in 1582 in the Finnish song collection *Piae Cantiones*. The lyrics may be based on a poem by Czech poet Václav Alois Svoboda. The lyrics portray St. Wenceslaus I, Duke of Bohemia (907—935). The Feast of St. Stephen falls upon December 26.

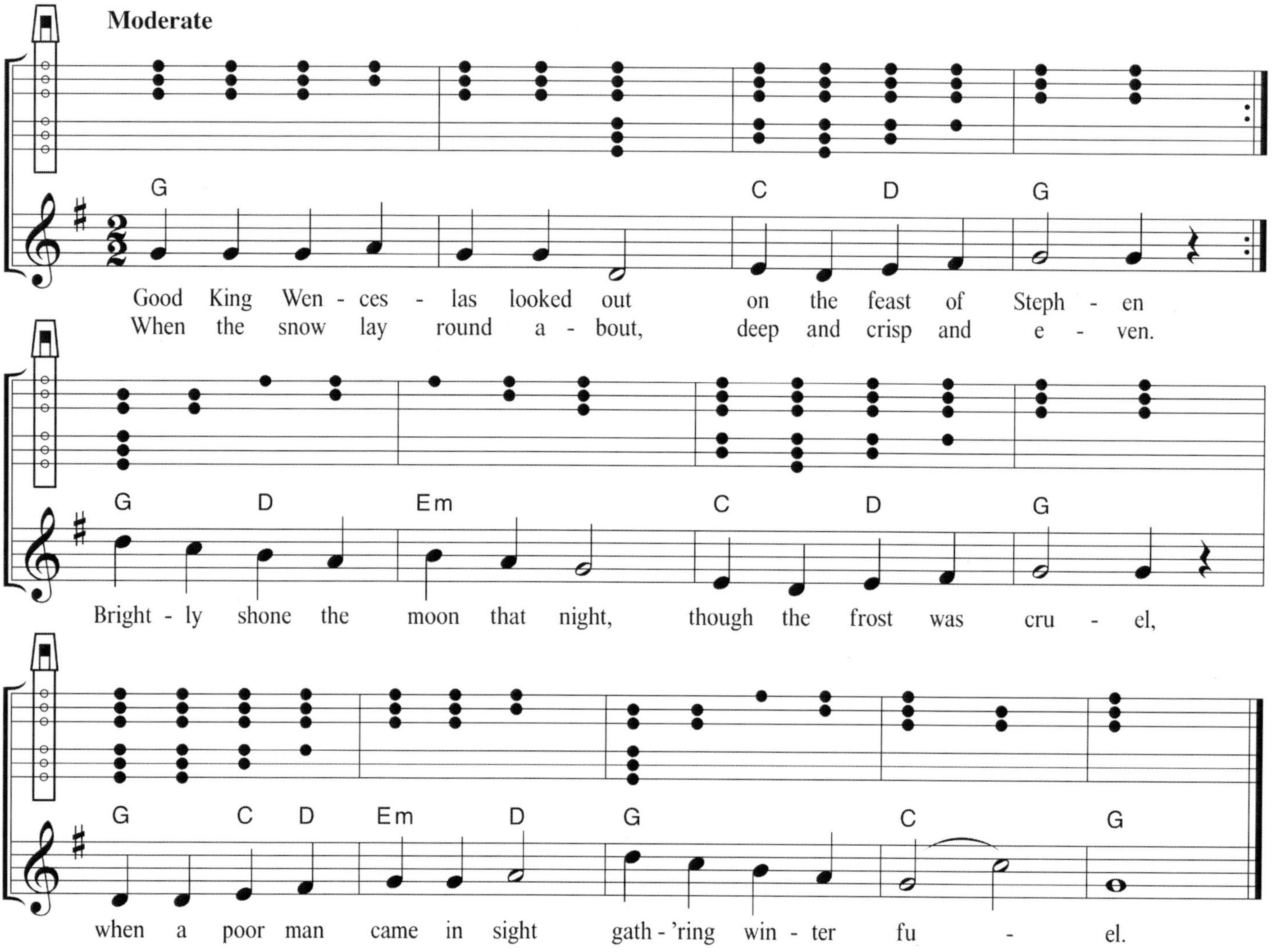

Hark! The Herald Angels Sing

The prolific English hymn writer Charles Wesley (1707—1788) wrote the lyrics to this carol. The melody, which became wedded to these words about 100 years later, was adapted from the 1840 *Festgesang* (also known as *The Gutenberg Cantata*) by German composer Felix Mendelssohn (1809—1847).

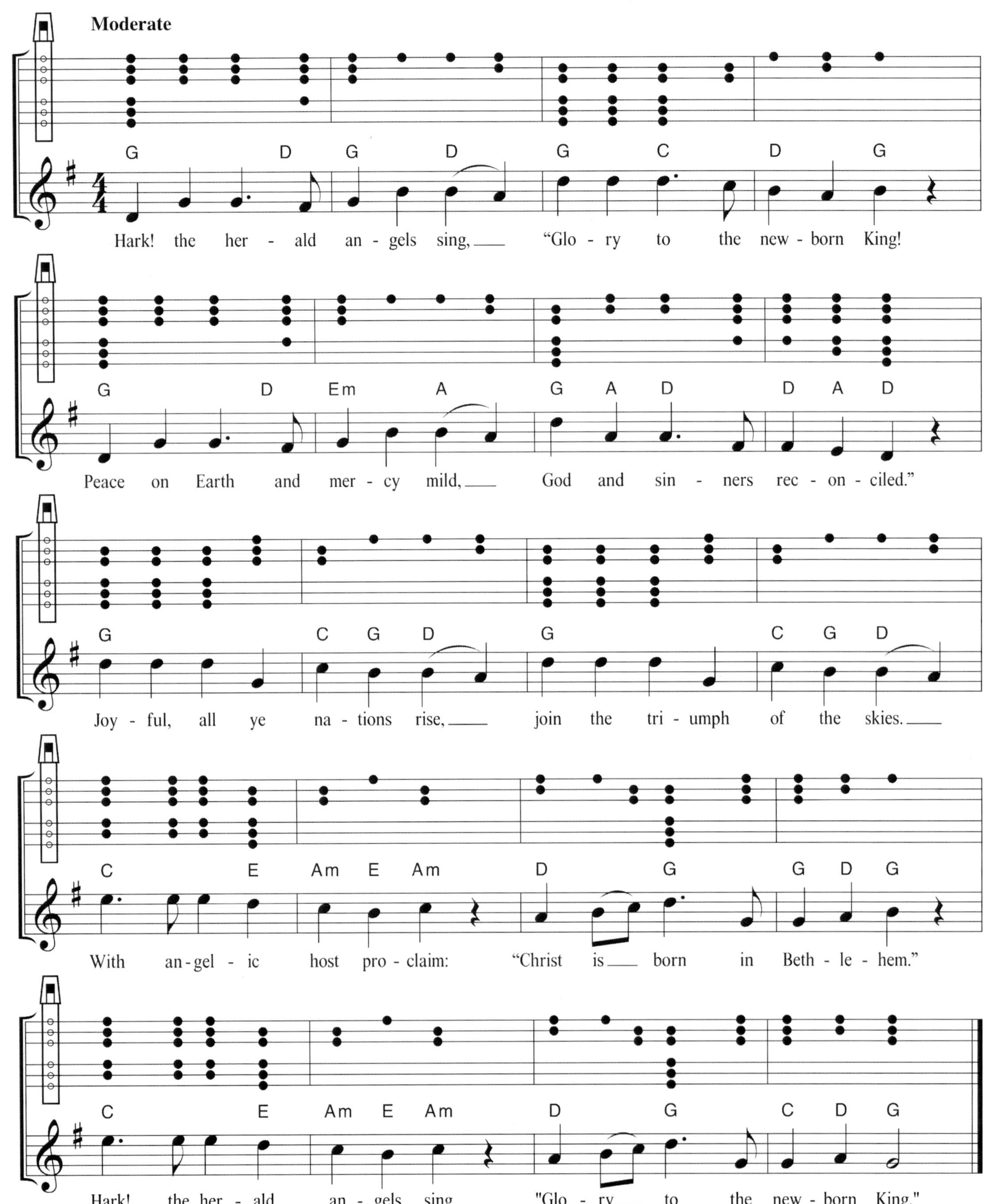

Here We Come A-Wassailing

This is a traditional carol and New Year's song from the north of England, thought to be composed c. 1850. Wassail is a spiced ale or mulled wine drunk during Christmas Eve and Twelfth Night celebrations. Wassailing carolers sang door to door, bestowing wishes of good health and often receiving food, drink or coins in return.

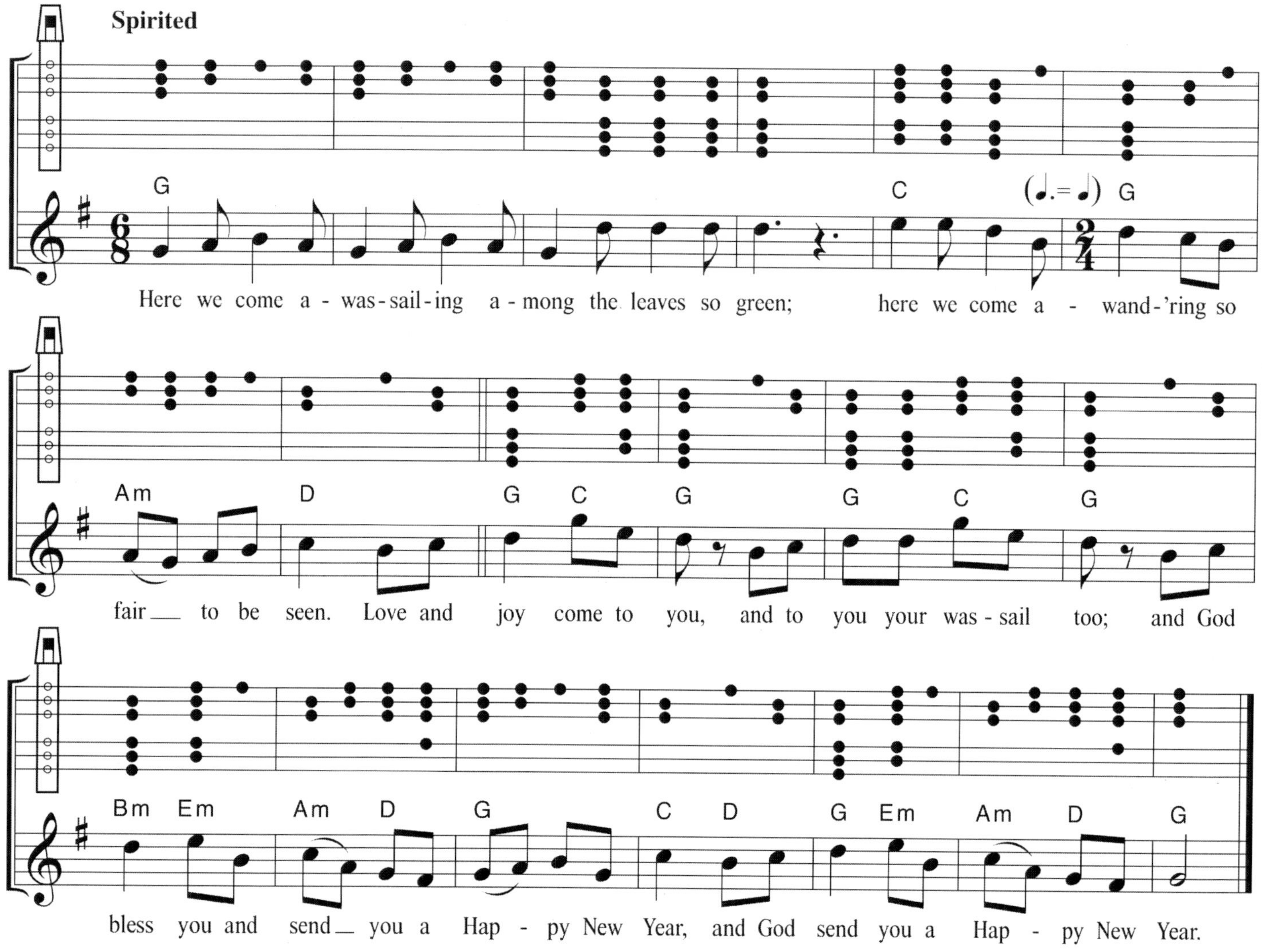

Spirited

G C (♩. = ♩) G

Here we come a - was-sail-ing a - mong the leaves so green; here we come a - wand-'ring so

Am D G C G G C G

fair__ to be seen. Love and joy come to you, and to you your was - sail too; and God

Bm Em Am D G C D G Em Am D G

bless you and send__ you a Hap - py New Year, and God send you a Hap - py New Year.

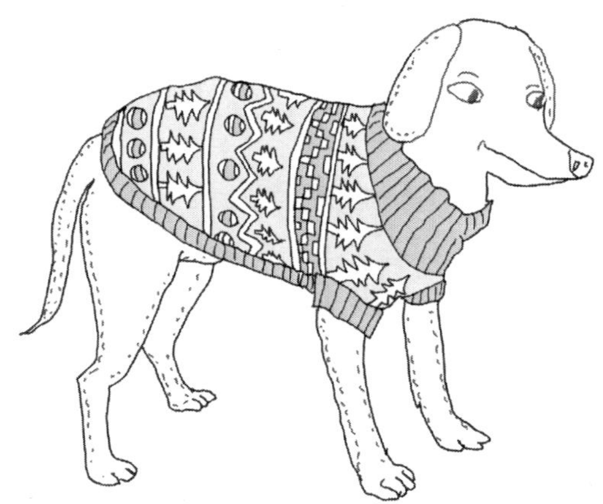

The Holly and the Ivy

This is an English folk carol. Its first known publication was in a broadside from c. 1710. The version widely known today was first published in 1911 by the English folksong collector Cecil Sharp in his *English Folk-Carols*. Holly and ivy were originally pagan symbols of masculinity and femininity, respectively, and later, in medieval times, came to symbolize Jesus and Mary.

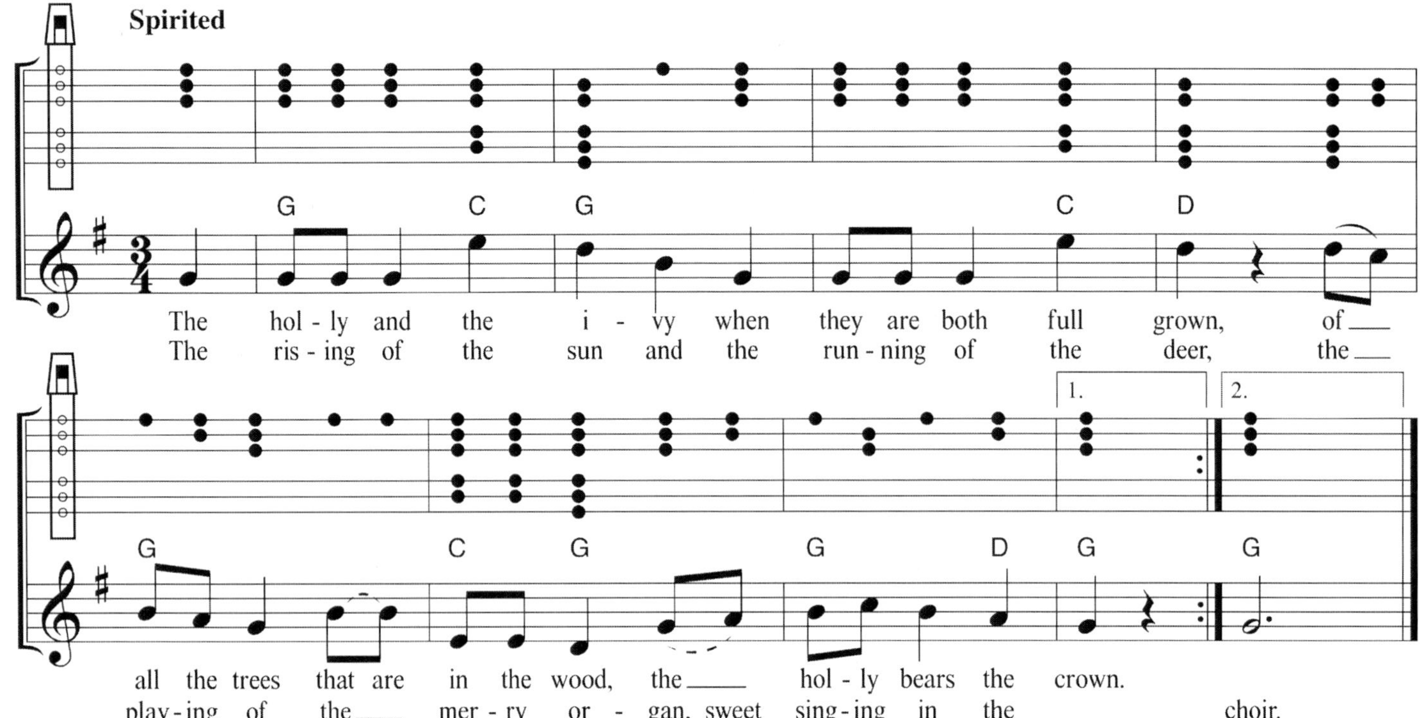

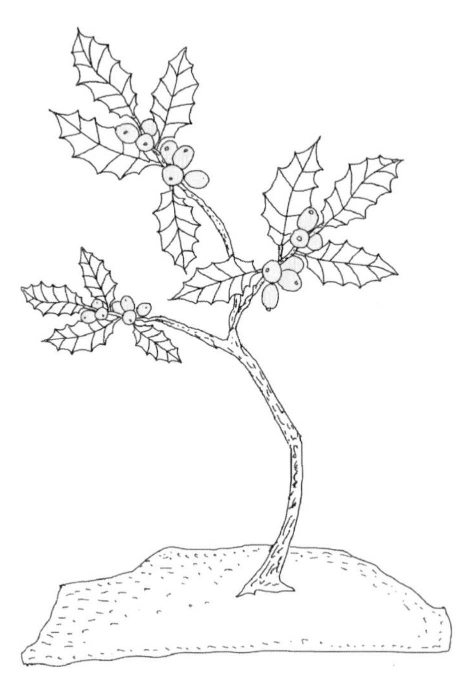

I Saw Three Ships

This is an English folk carol. The earliest printed version appeared on a broadside from the 17th century, possibly from Derbyshire. The three ships are thought to symbolize either the Biblical Magis' camels (known as "ships of the desert"), the three ships which carried the purported relics of the Magi to the Cologne Cathedral in 1162, or the ships on the coat of arms of St. Wenceslaus of Bohemia. (See "Good King Wenceslas.")

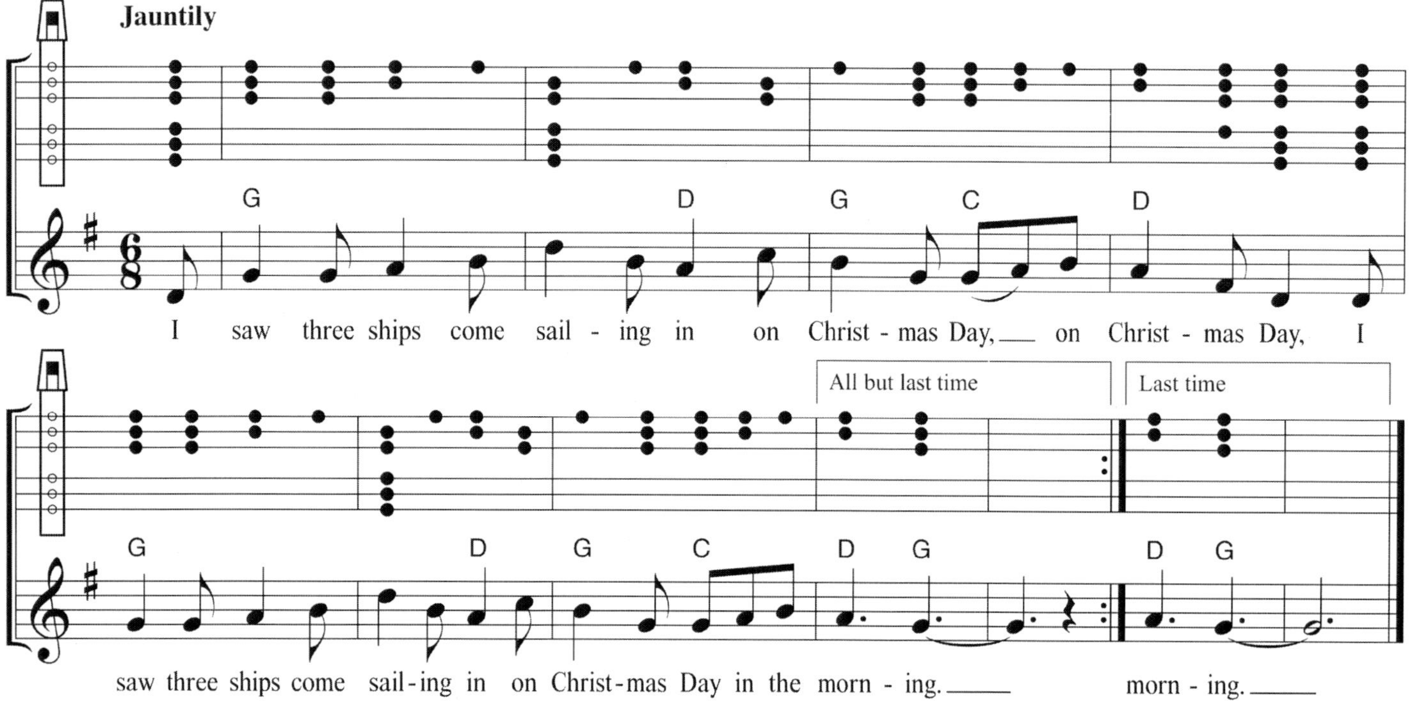

In the Bleak Midwinter

The lyrics of this carol are based upon an 1872 poem by the English poet Christina Rossetti (1830—1894). There have been numerous musical settings, but the one given here, and most widely known today, was composed by the English composer Gustav Holst (1874—1934) for the 1906 edition of *The English Hymnal*.

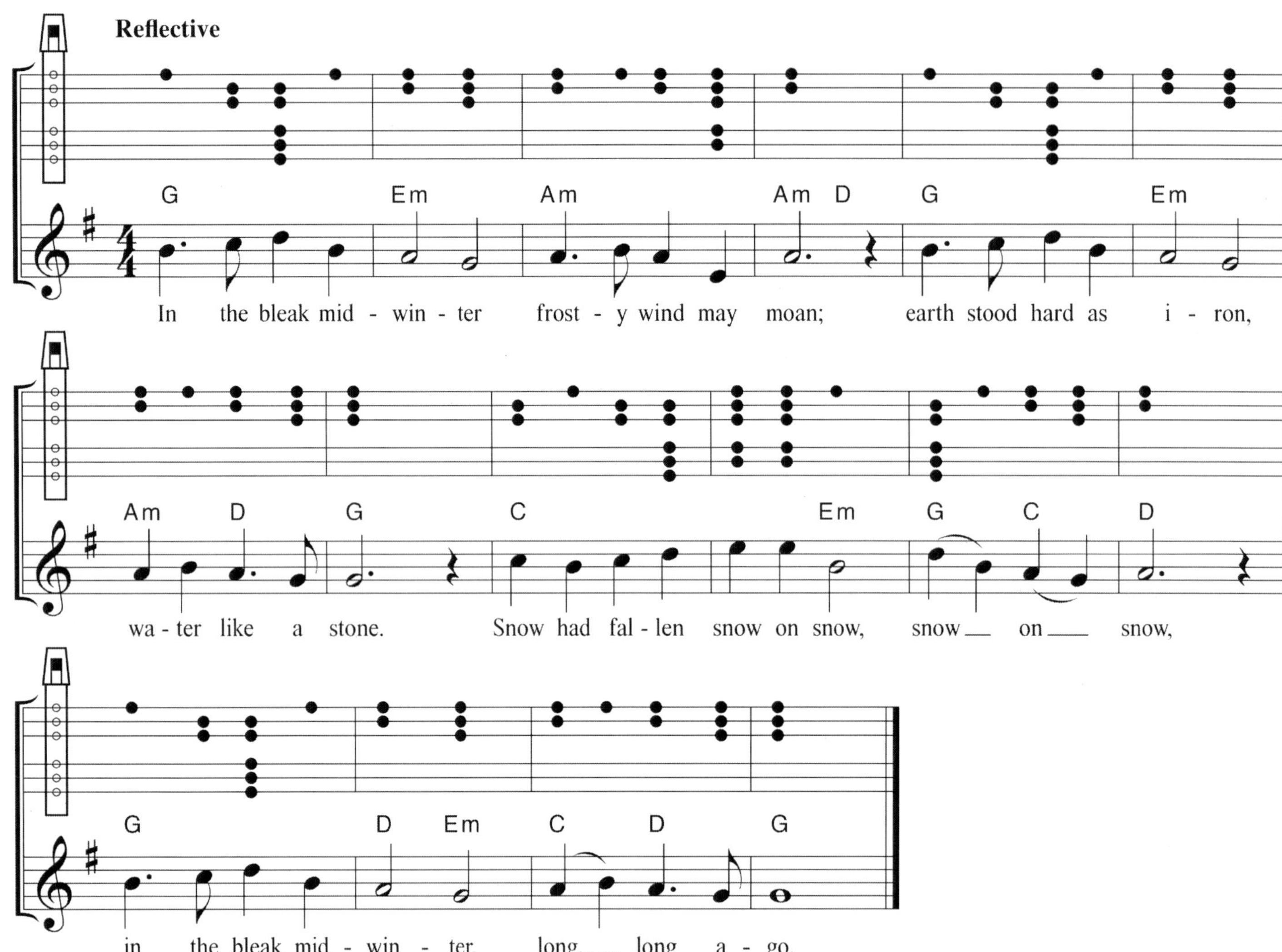

Jingle Bells

James Pierpont (1822—1893), an American, wrote this song c. 1850. He intended it for Thanksgiving, but soon it became widely associated with Christmas. In New England people often put bells on horses' harnesses as a way to avoid collisions at blind intersections, since a horse-drawn sleigh in snow makes almost no sound.

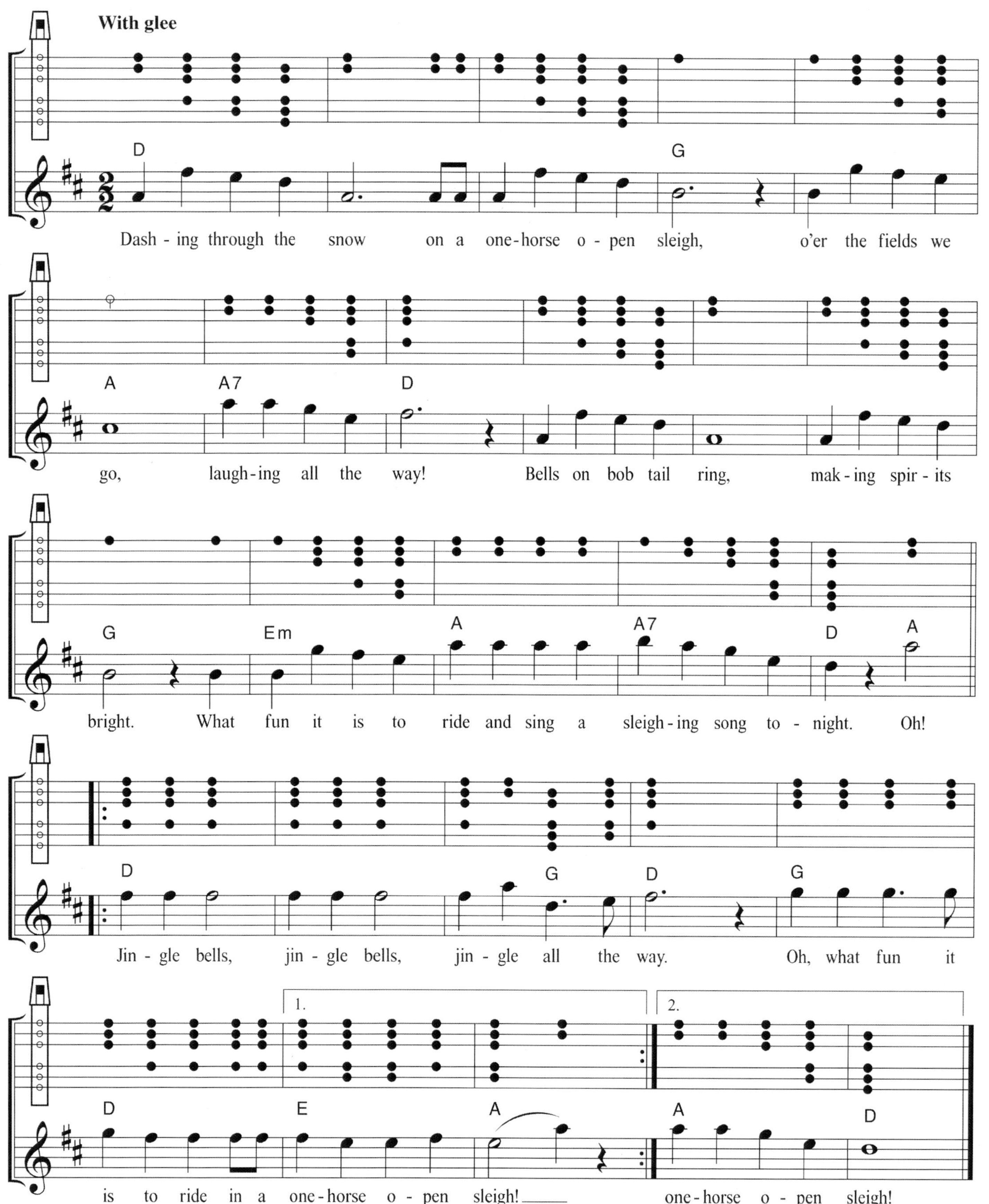

Jolly Old St. Nicholas

The lyrics to this American Christmas song are based on the 1865 poem "Lilly's Secret" by Emily Huntington Miller (1833—1913). The melody has been attributed to John Piersol McCaskey (1837—1935) of Lancaster, Pennsylvania. The "Johnny" mentioned in the song was McCaskey's son, who died as a child.

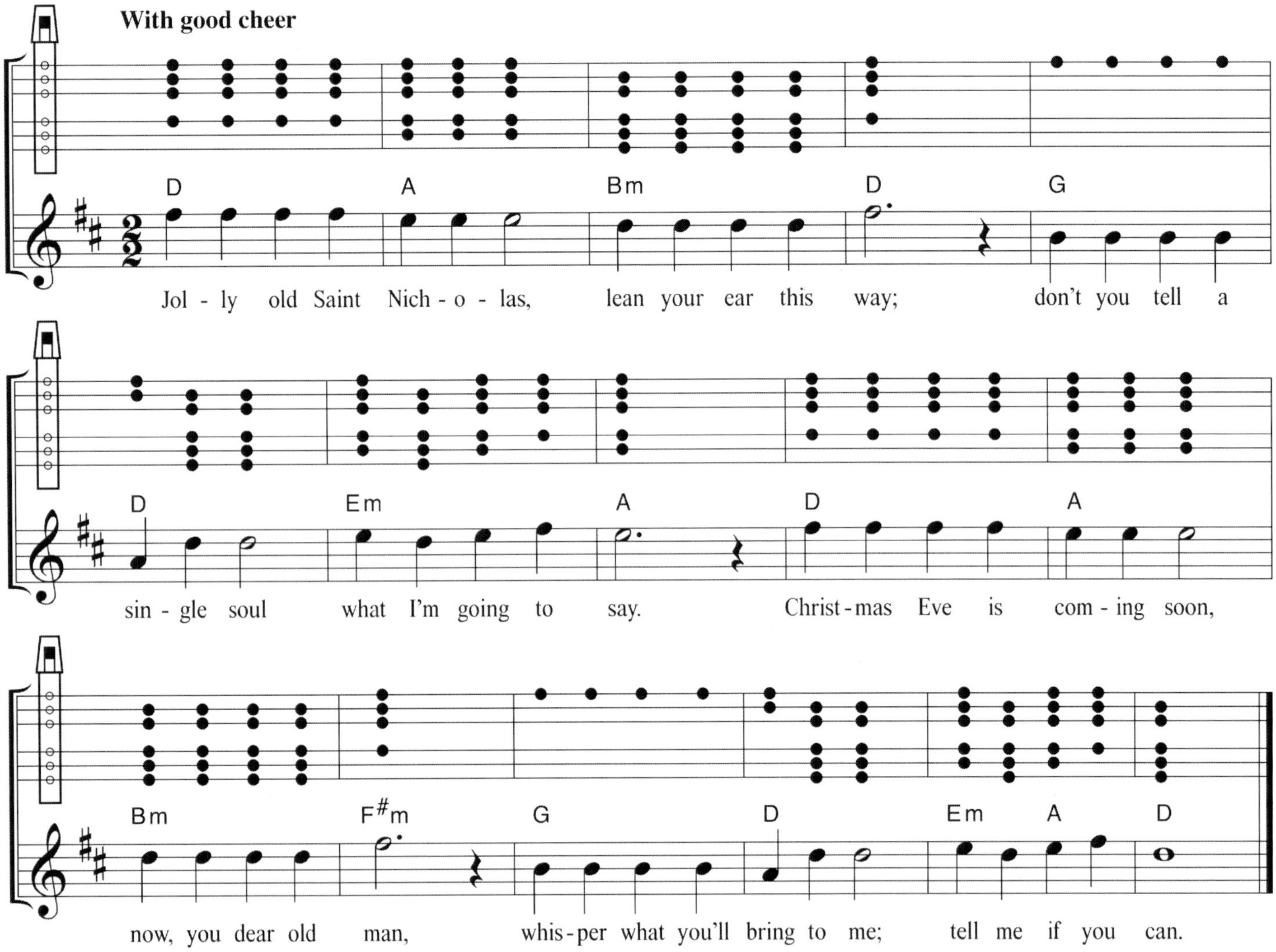

With good cheer

D A Bm D G

Jol - ly old Saint Nich - o - las, lean your ear this way; don't you tell a

D Em A D A

sin - gle soul what I'm going to say. Christ - mas Eve is com - ing soon,

Bm F#m G D Em A D

now, you dear old man, whis - per what you'll bring to me; tell me if you can.

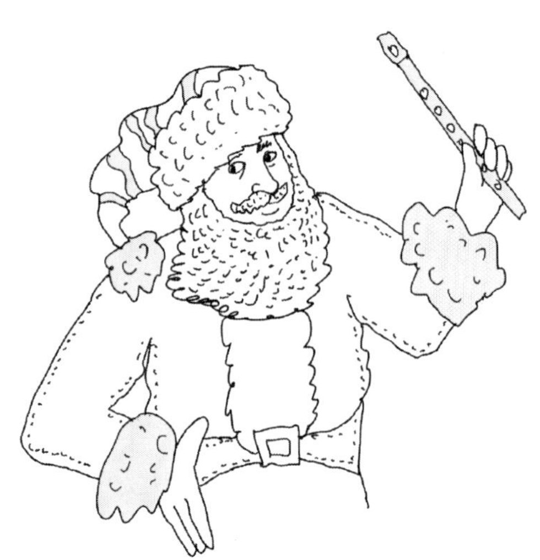

Joy to the World

The English poet Issac Watts (1675—1748) wrote the lyrics to this carol and published them in 1719. The melody's origin is unclear, but it may be an amalgamation of several hymn tunes. The opinion that the melody is derived from music written by George Frideric Handel (1685—1759) has been disputed by Handel scholars.

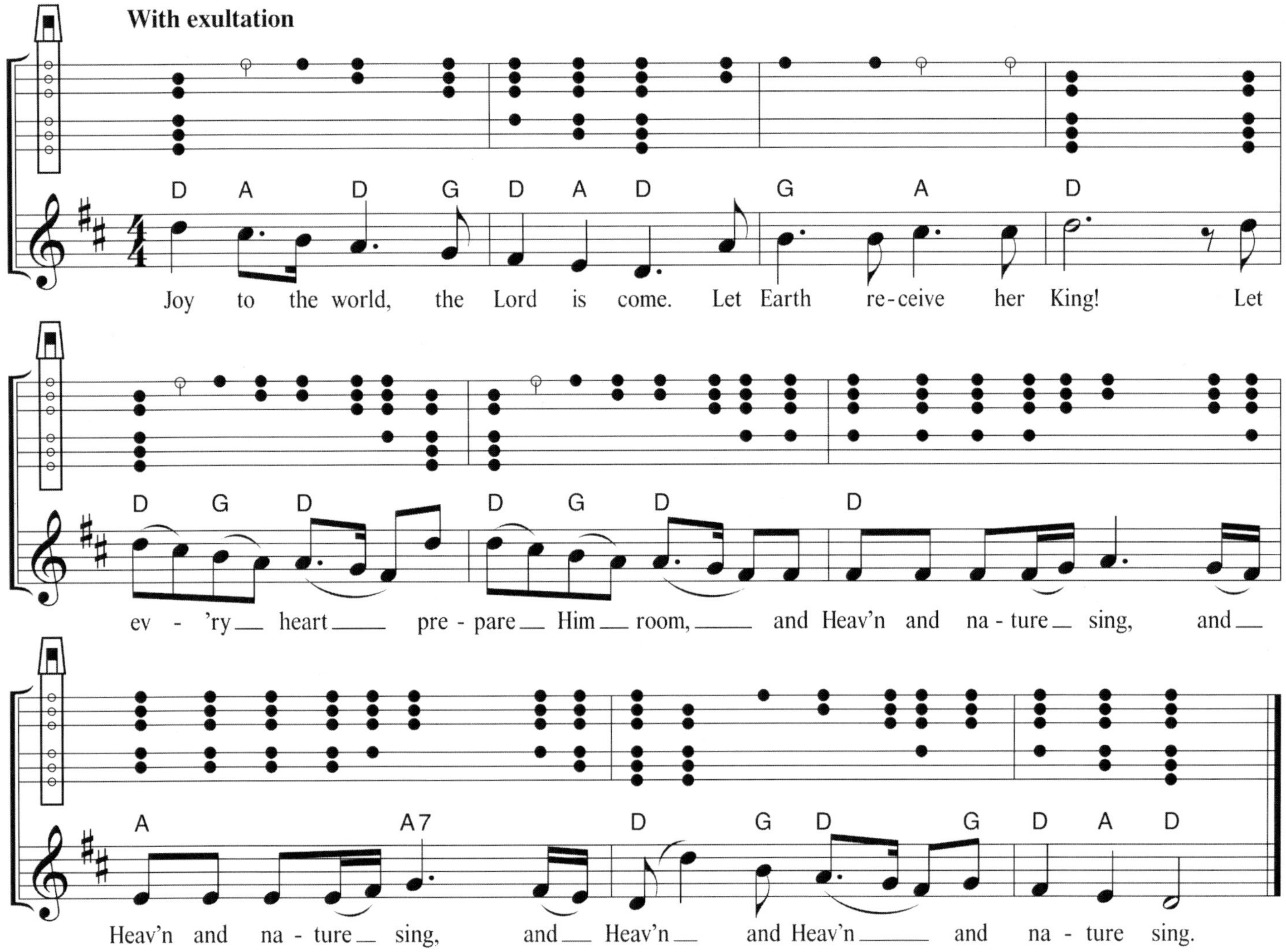

With exultation

D A D G D A D G A D

Joy to the world, the Lord is come. Let Earth re-ceive her King! Let

D G D D G D D

ev - 'ry heart pre - pare Him room, and Heav'n and na - ture sing, and

A A7 D G D G D A D

Heav'n and na - ture sing, and Heav'n and Heav'n and na - ture sing.

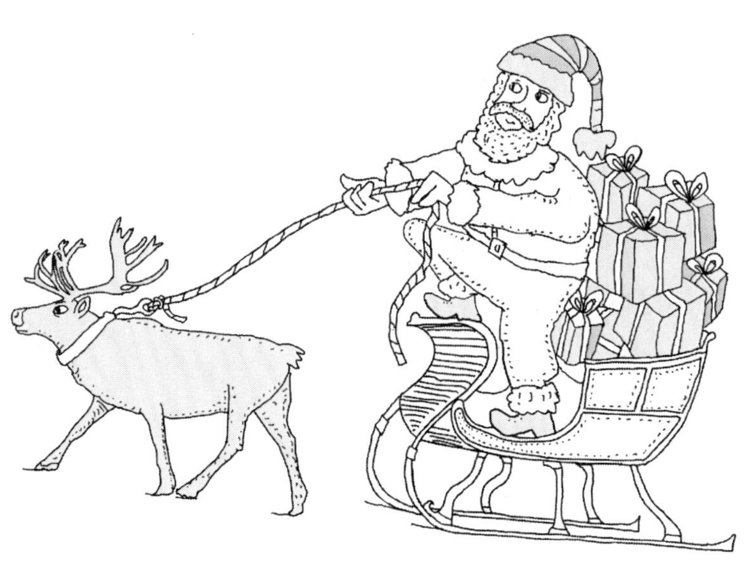

Lo, How a Rose E'er Blooming

The lyrics to this German carol and hymn, "Es ist ein Ros entsprungen," date from the 15th century. The melody in common use today first appeared in print in 1599 and was harmonized by the German composer Michael Praetorius (1571—1621) in 1609. The rose in the lyrics symbolizes the Virgin Mary.

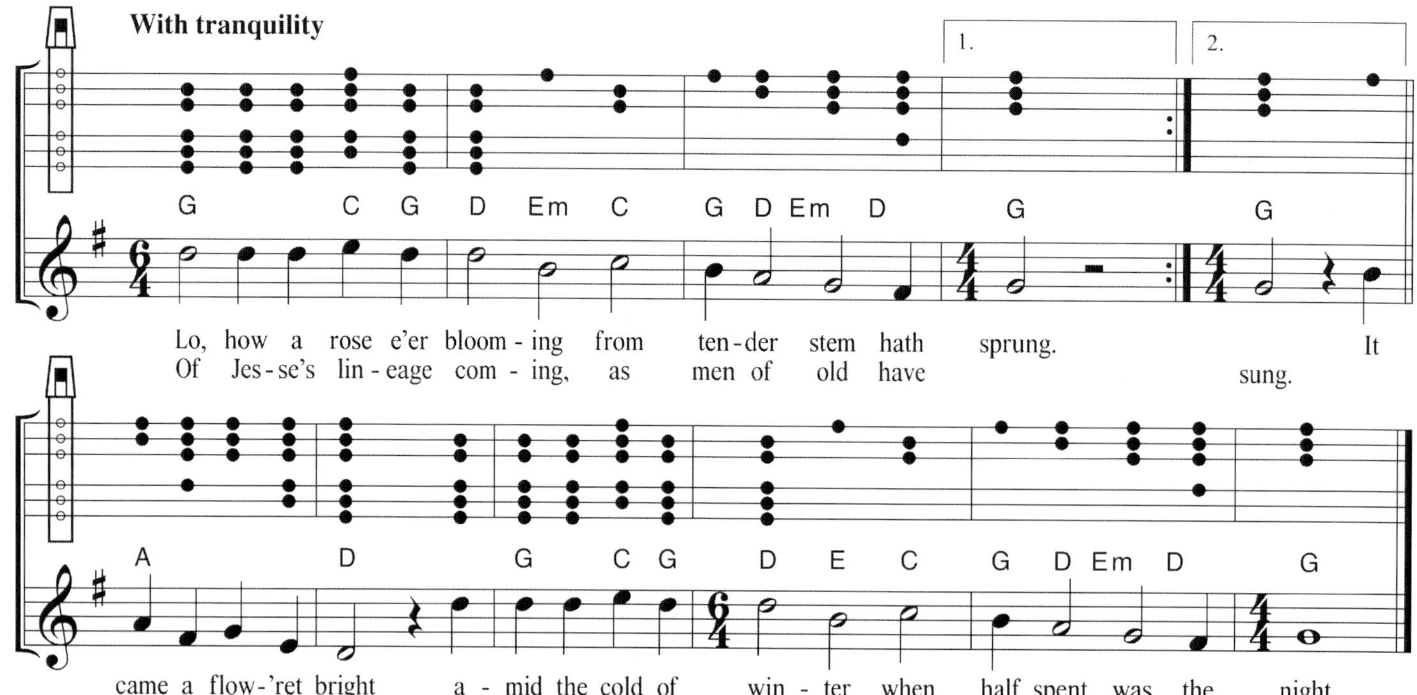

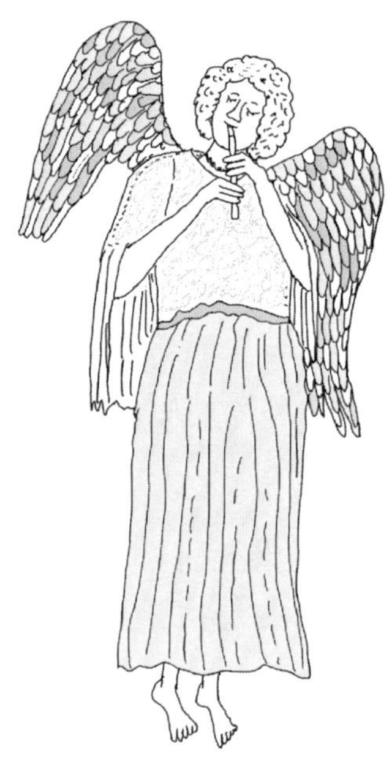

O Christmas Tree

The German folksong "O Tannenbaum" dates from the 16th century. In 1824, Ernst Anschütz added to the traditional first verse, which refers neither to Christmas nor a decorated tree, but instead to the evergreen as a symbol of constancy and faithfulness. Anschütz's new verses engendered the association with Christmas.

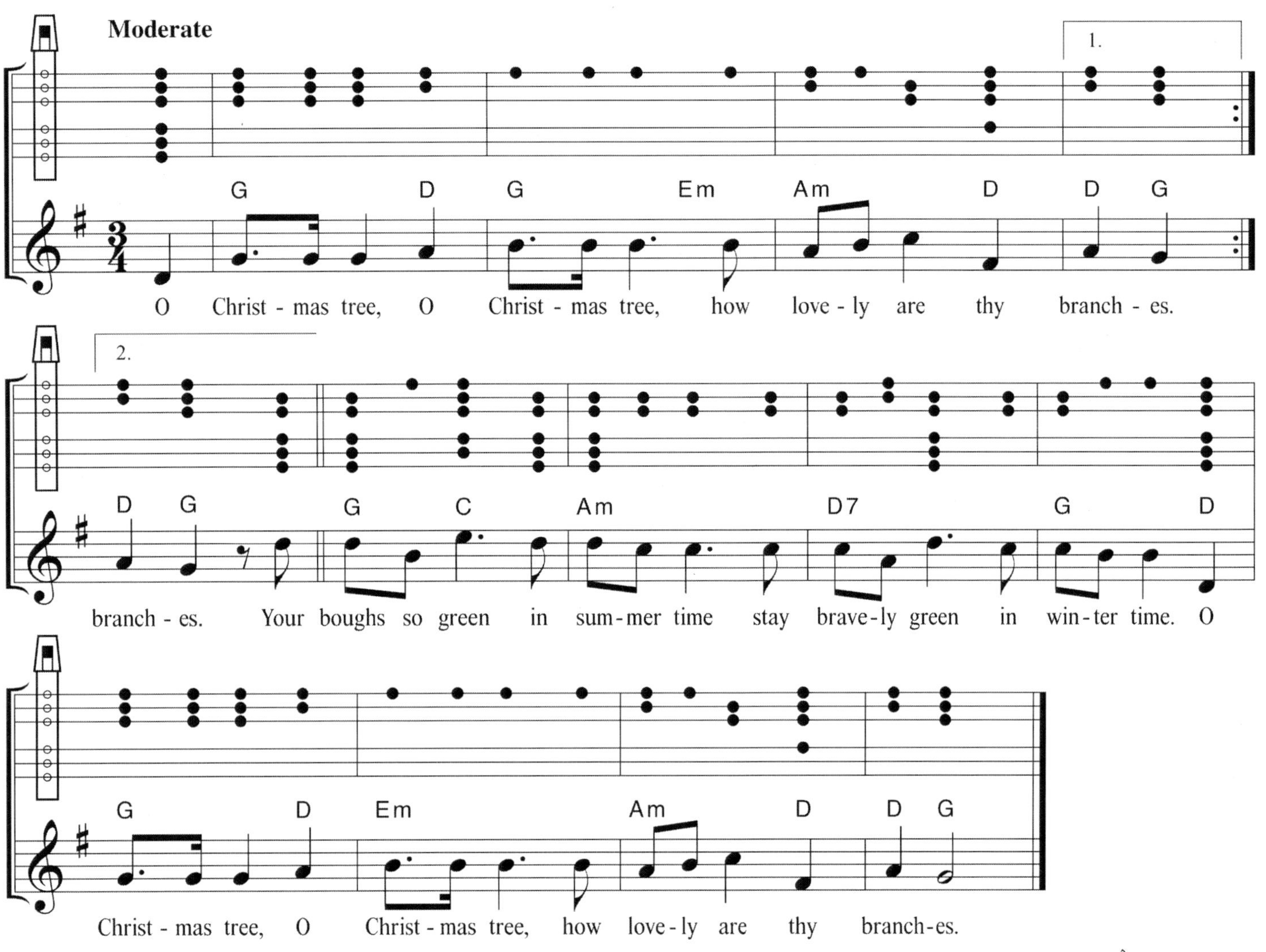

O Come, All Ye Faithful

The carol "Adeste Fideles" was first published in England in 1782. The melody was probably written in 1751 by Englishman John Francis Wade (1711—1786) while he was living in exile in France. The lyrics, written in Latin, may date back as far as the 13th century. King John IV of Portugal (1604—1656) held the oldest known manuscript of these lyrics, dated 1640, in his palace at Via Viçosa, Portugal.

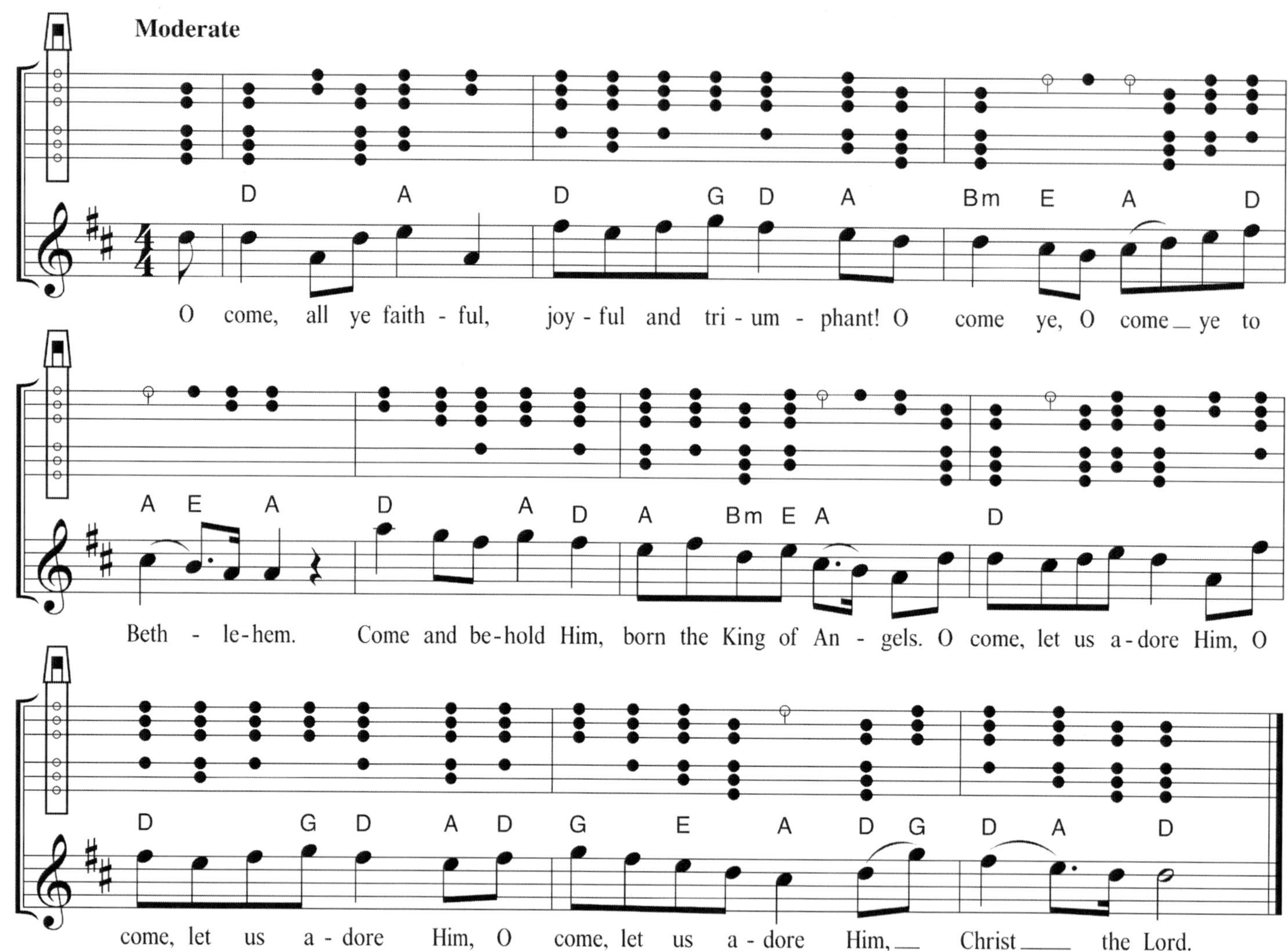

O Come, Little Children

The lyrics to the German Christmas carol "Ihr Kinderlien, kommet" were written in 1798 by Catholic priest Christoph von Schmid (1785—1854). The melody in common use today was composed in 1790 by Johann Abraham Peter Schulz (1747—1800) as a secular song called "Wie reizend, wie wonnig" (How Charming, How Pleasant). The carol was first published with this melody in Germany c. 1832.

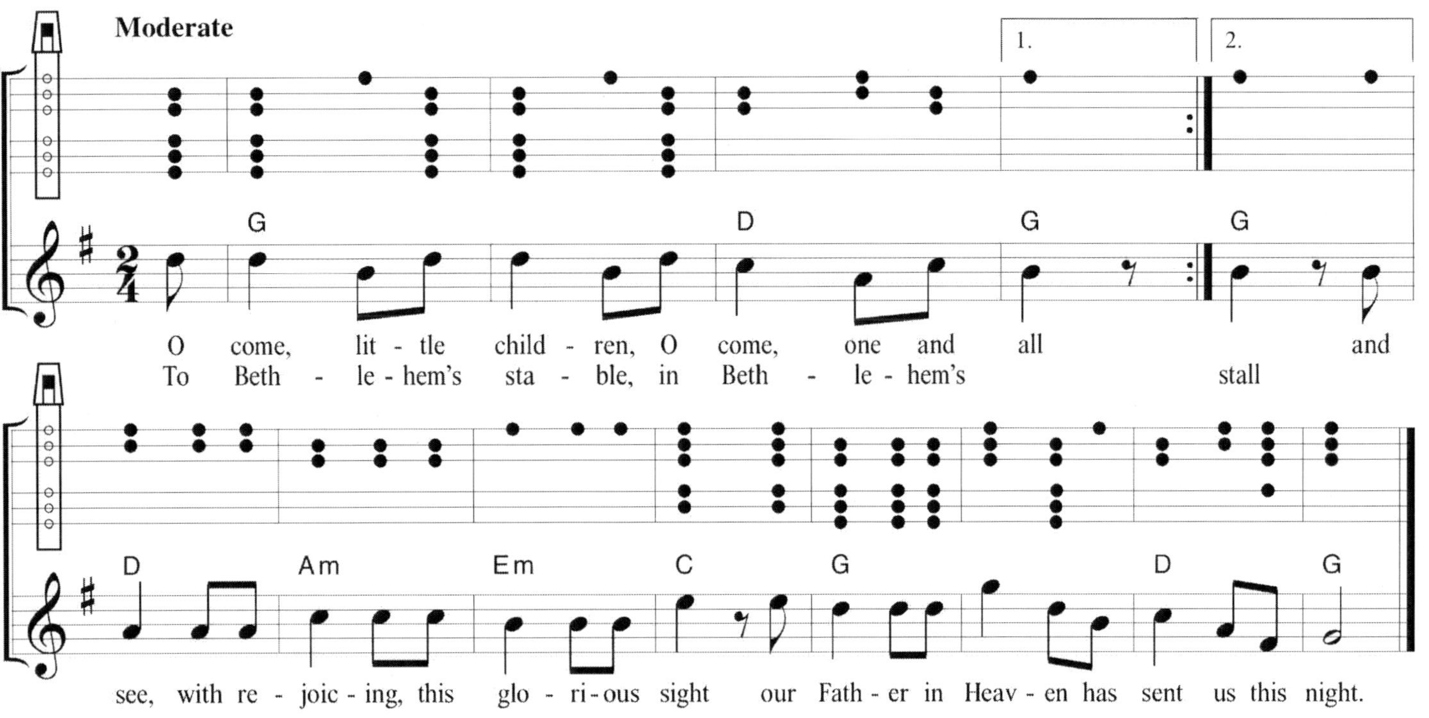

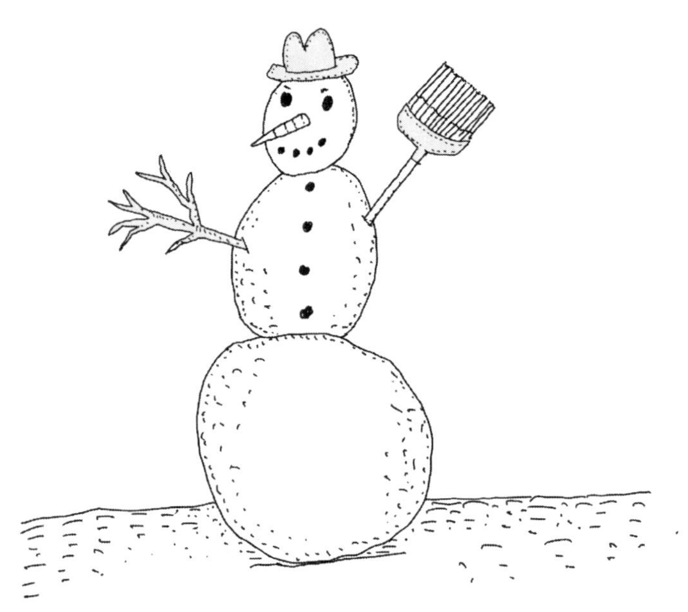

O Come, O Come, Emmanuel

The words and music to the Christmas hymn "Veni, veni Emmanuel" evolved separately. The Latin lyrics were first documented in Germany in 1710 but are rooted in texts from the eighth century or earlier. The melody has its origins in 15th century France. The melody and lyrics, in both Latin and English, were first published together in England in 1851 by John Mason Neale (1818—1866).

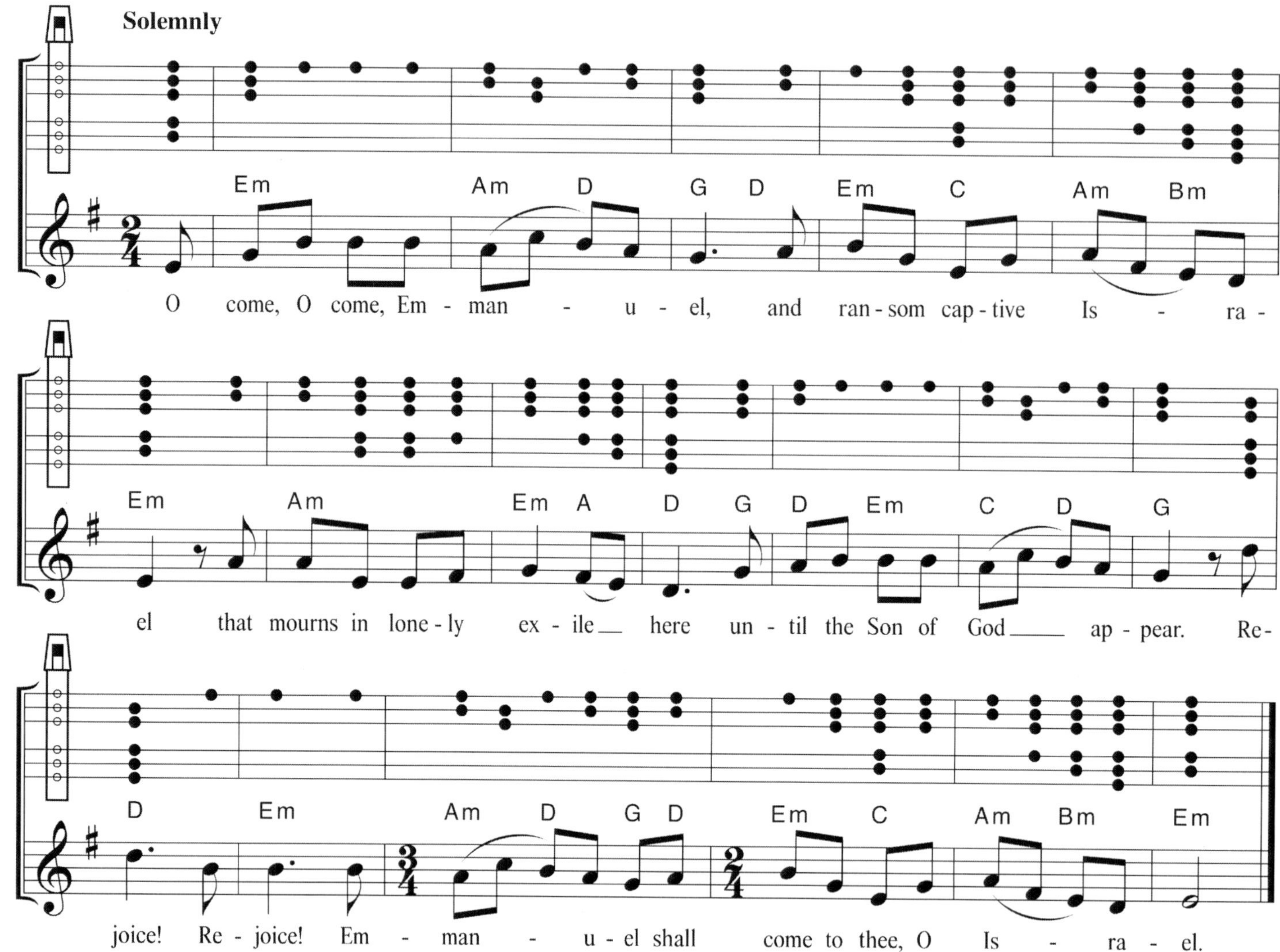

Silent Night

The lyrics to "Stille Nacht, heilige Nacht" were written in 1816 by a young Austrian priest, Joseph Mohr (1792—1848). In 1818, Mohr asked Franz Xaver Gruber (1787—1863), organist at St. Nicholas church in Oberndorf, to write a melody, along with guitar accompaniment, for Christmas Eve Mass, as the organ had been damaged in a flood. The organ repairman spread the song far and wide, leading to its immense popularity today.

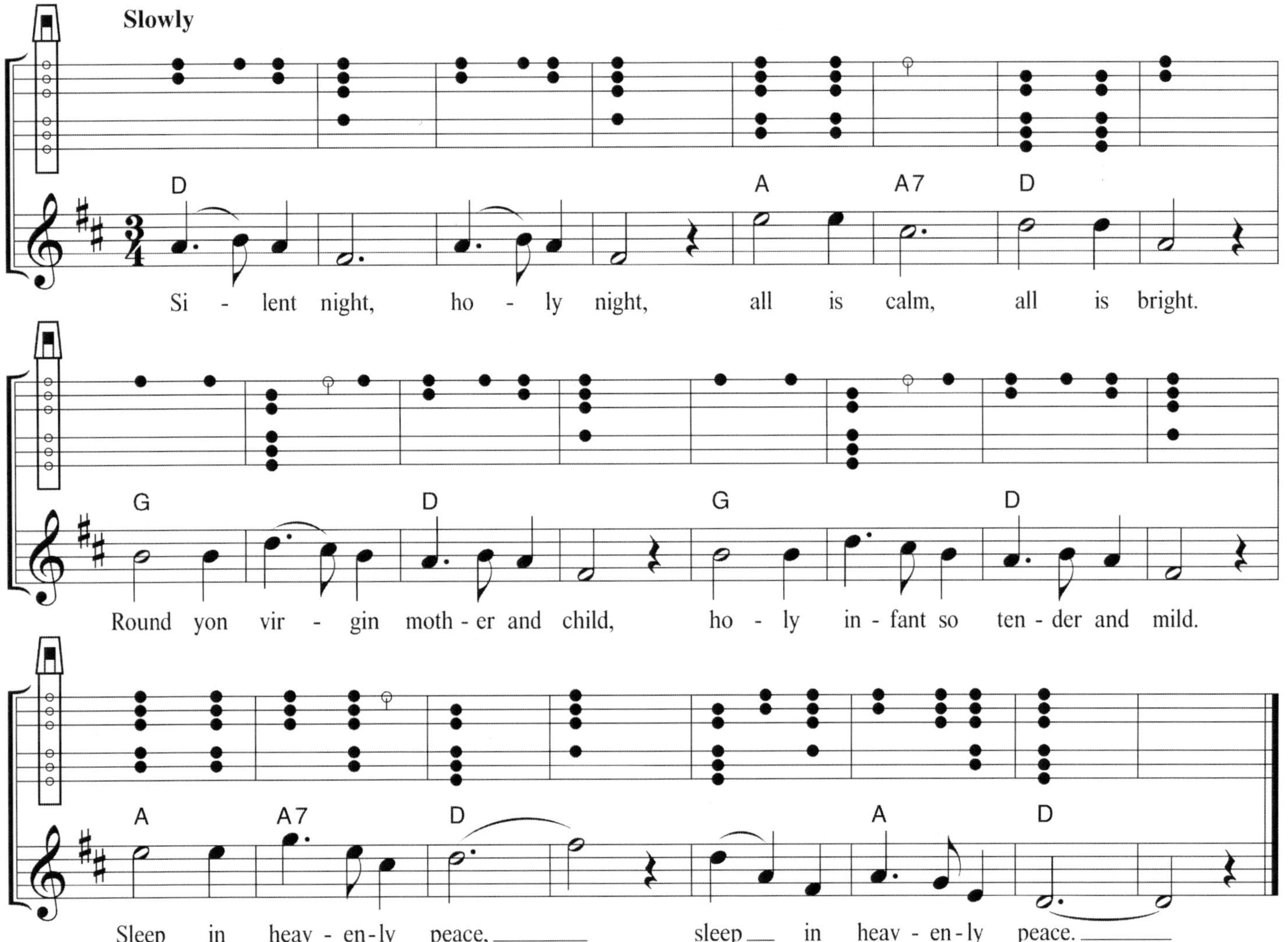

Sing We Now of Christmas

The French Christmas and New Year's carol "Noël nouvelet" dates from the 15th century. It was likely sung by families at home and at community gatherings and not as part of the Catholic liturgy. English translations appear as early as the 17th century. The melody is in the Dorian mode and shares its first five notes with the Marian hymn "Ave, Maris Stella Lucens Miseris."

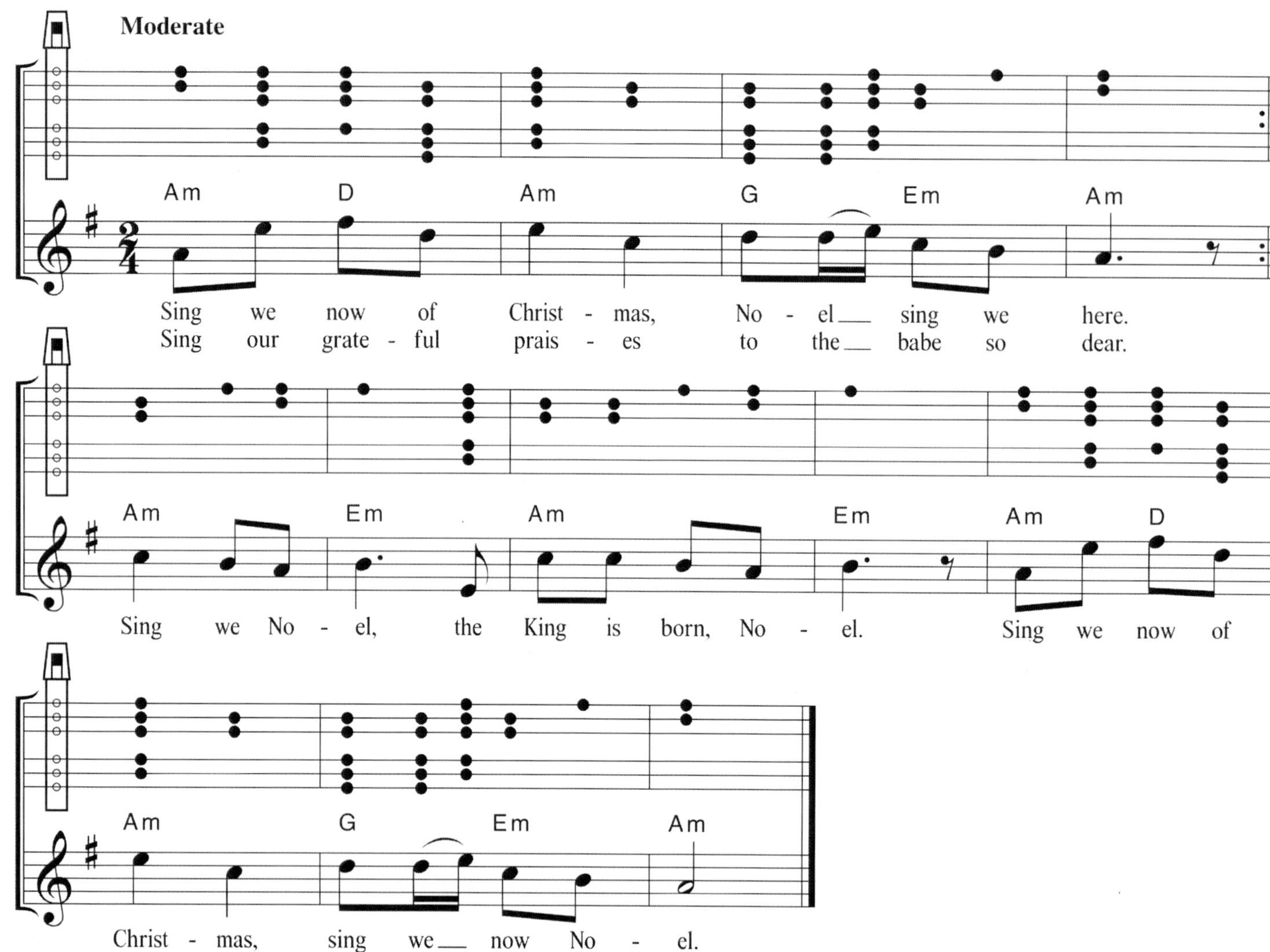

The Snow Lay on the Ground

This appears to be a traditional Irish Christmas carol, with lyrics in Irish and Latin. The English translation of the Irish lyrics is credited to the English historian and Catholic priest John Lingard (1771—1851). Lingard wrote the popular Marian hymn "Hail, Queen of Heaven, the Ocean Star" which may have influenced J. R. R. Tolkien's writing of the Elvish hymn "A Elbereth Gilthoniel," found in *The Lord of the Rings*.

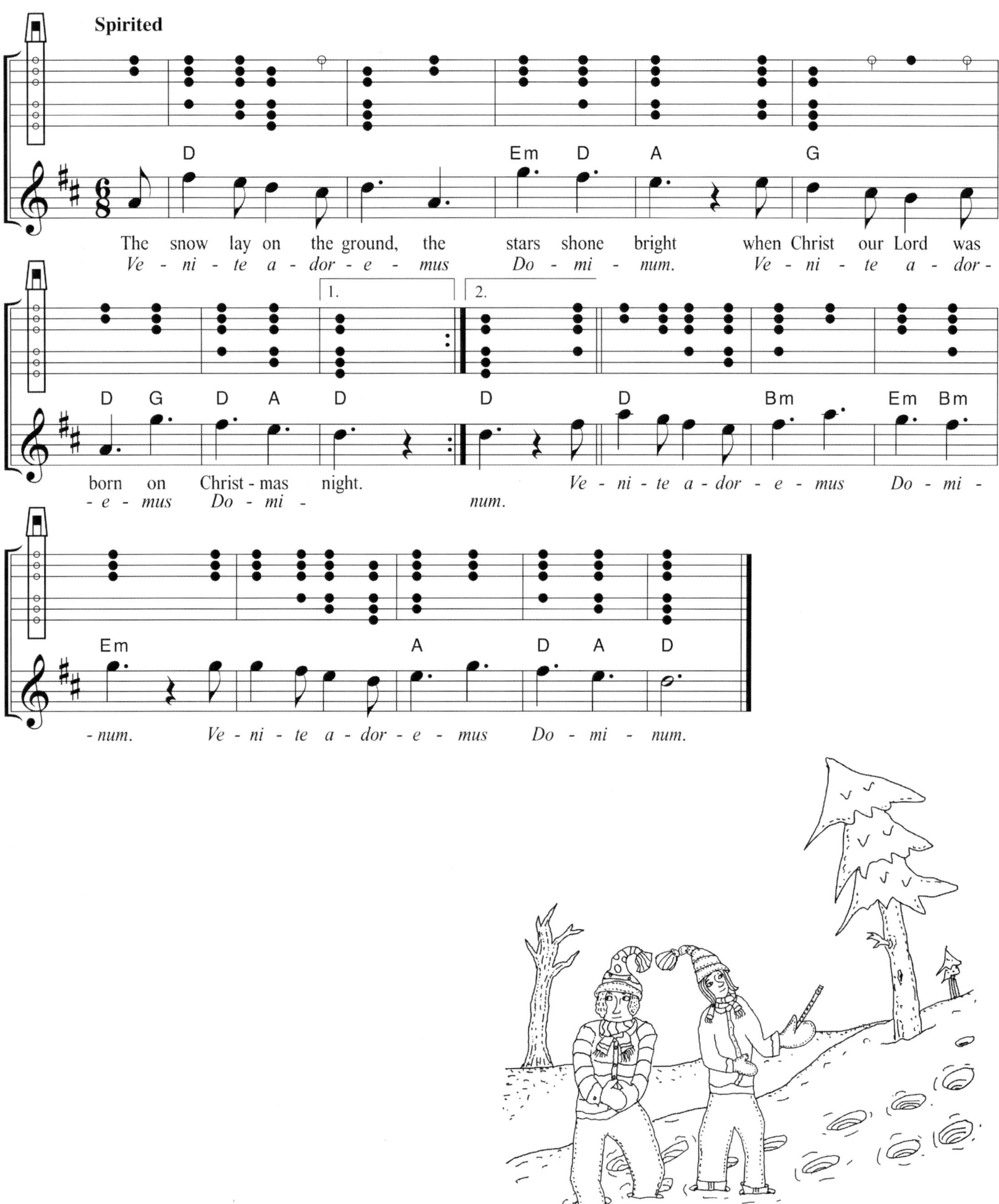

The Twelve Days of Christmas

It is not known whether this Christmas carol, a song of cumulative gift giving, is of English or French origin. The lyrics were first published in England in 1780 in a children's book, *Mirth without Mischief*, as a memorization game to be played on Twelfth Night (the fifth of January).

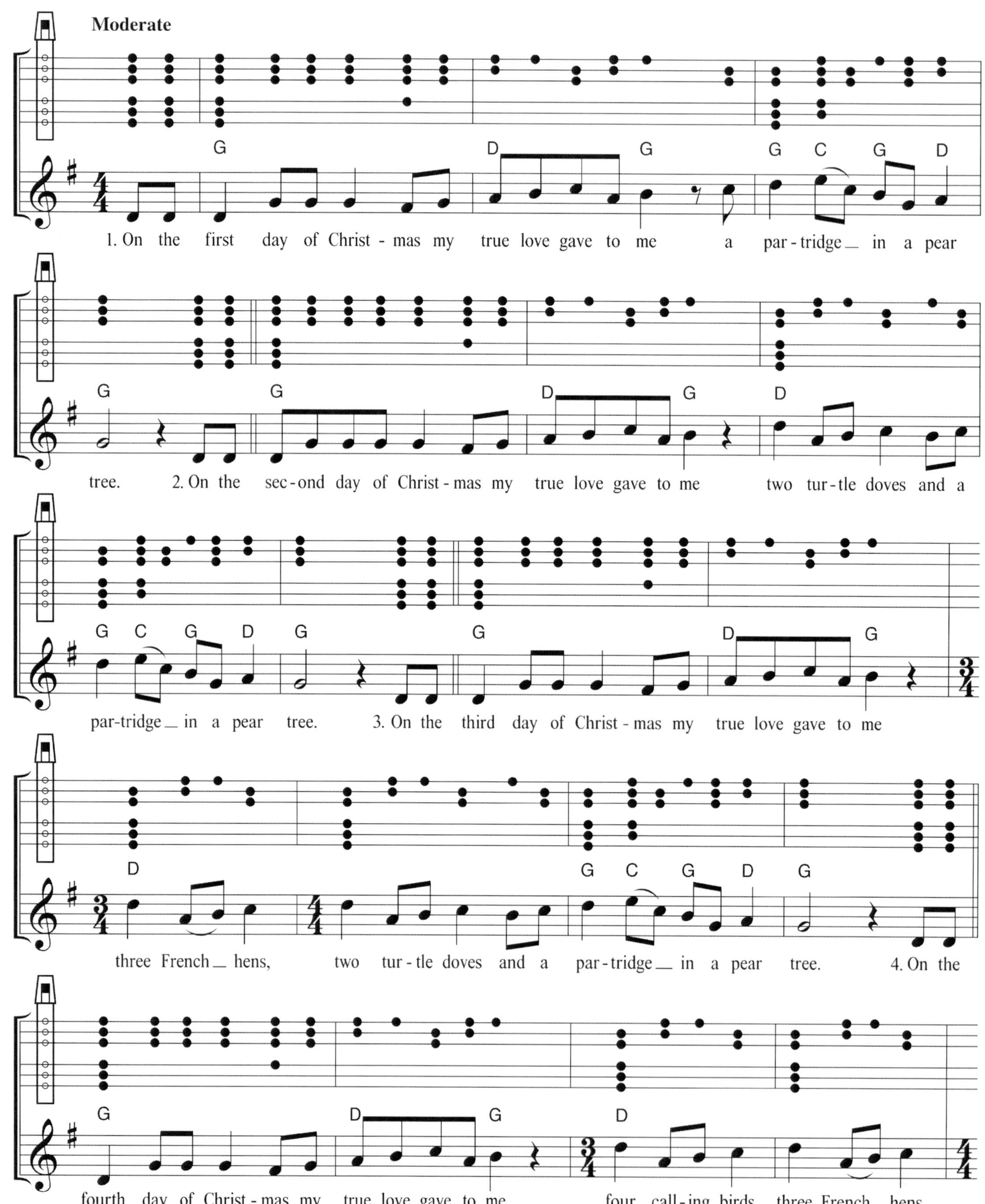

The Twelve Days of Christmas, continued

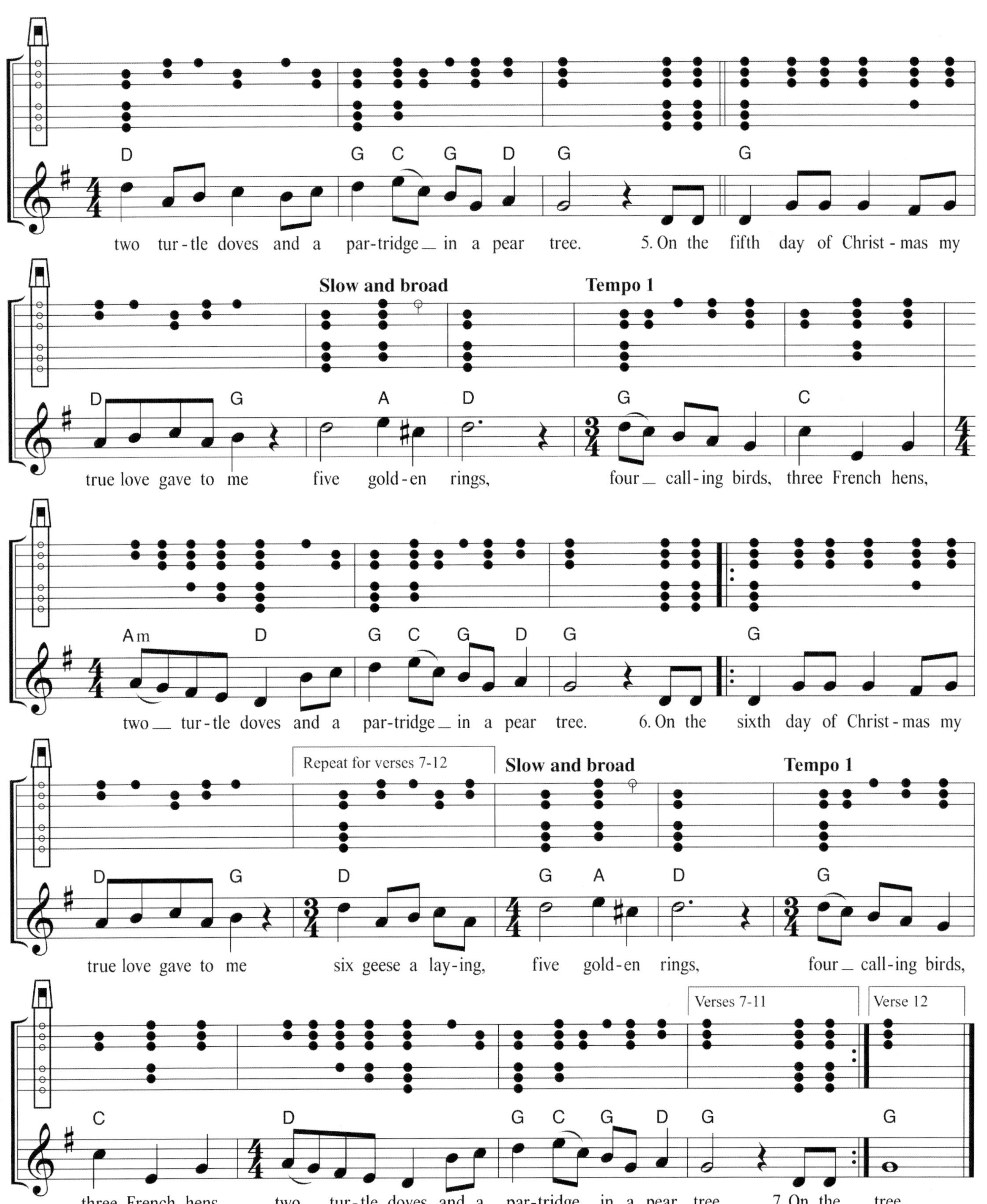

Up on the Housetop

This song was written by American composer, educator and pastor Benjamin Russel Hanby (1833—1867) as a Christmas sing-along. It is considered to be one of the first secular Christmas songs, and the earliest one to focus primarily on Santa Claus. A native of Ohio, Hanby wrote some 80 songs, including "Darling Nelly Gray." He operated a singing school, and he and his father were active with the Underground Railroad.

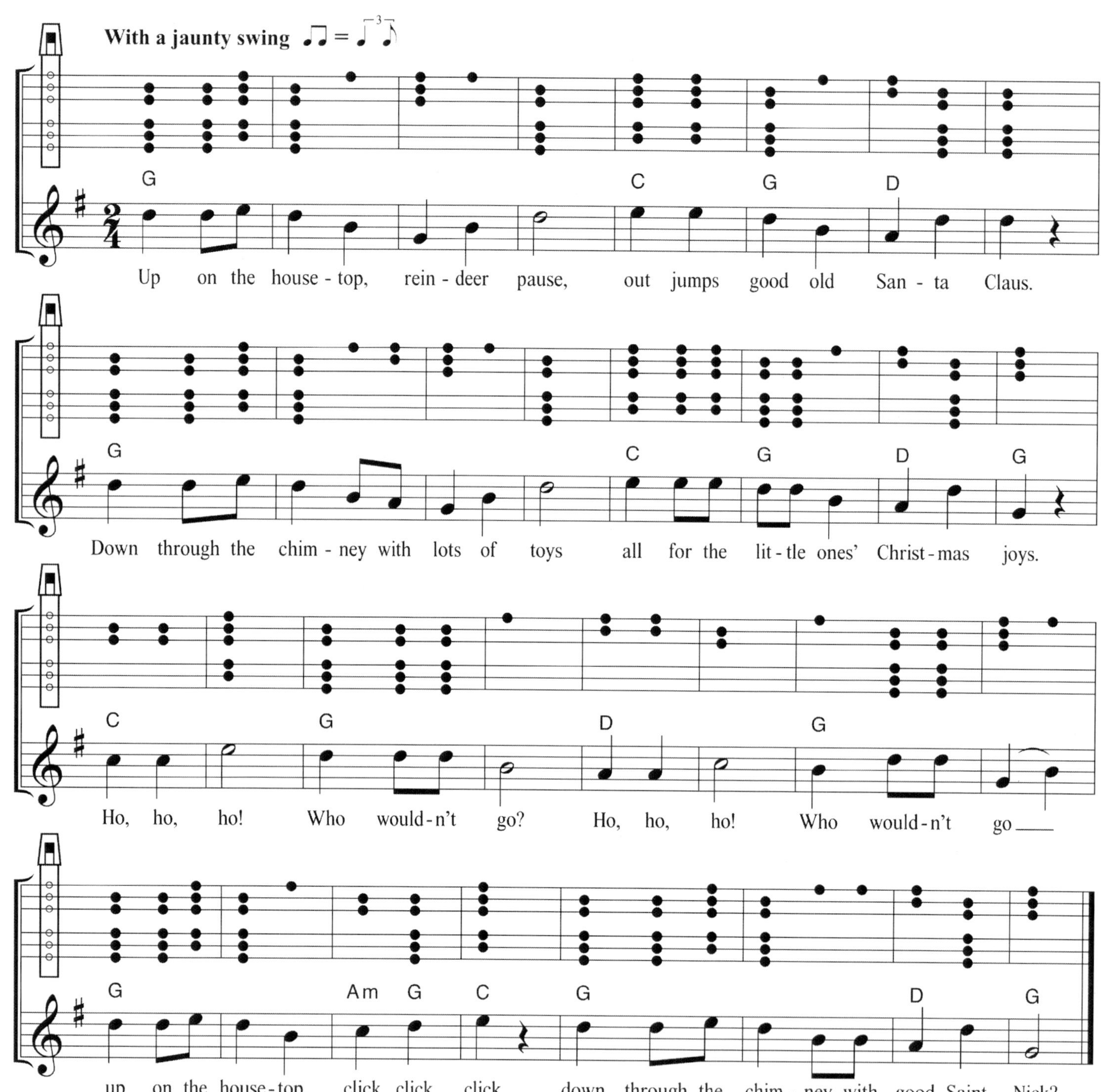

We Three Kings

John Henry Hopkins, rector of Christ Episcopal Church in Williamsport, Pennsylvania, wrote the words and music to this American Christmas carol in 1857. It was performed that year for a Christmas pageant at the General Theological Seminary in New York City, where Hopkins also taught music. The song went on to achieve international acclaim.

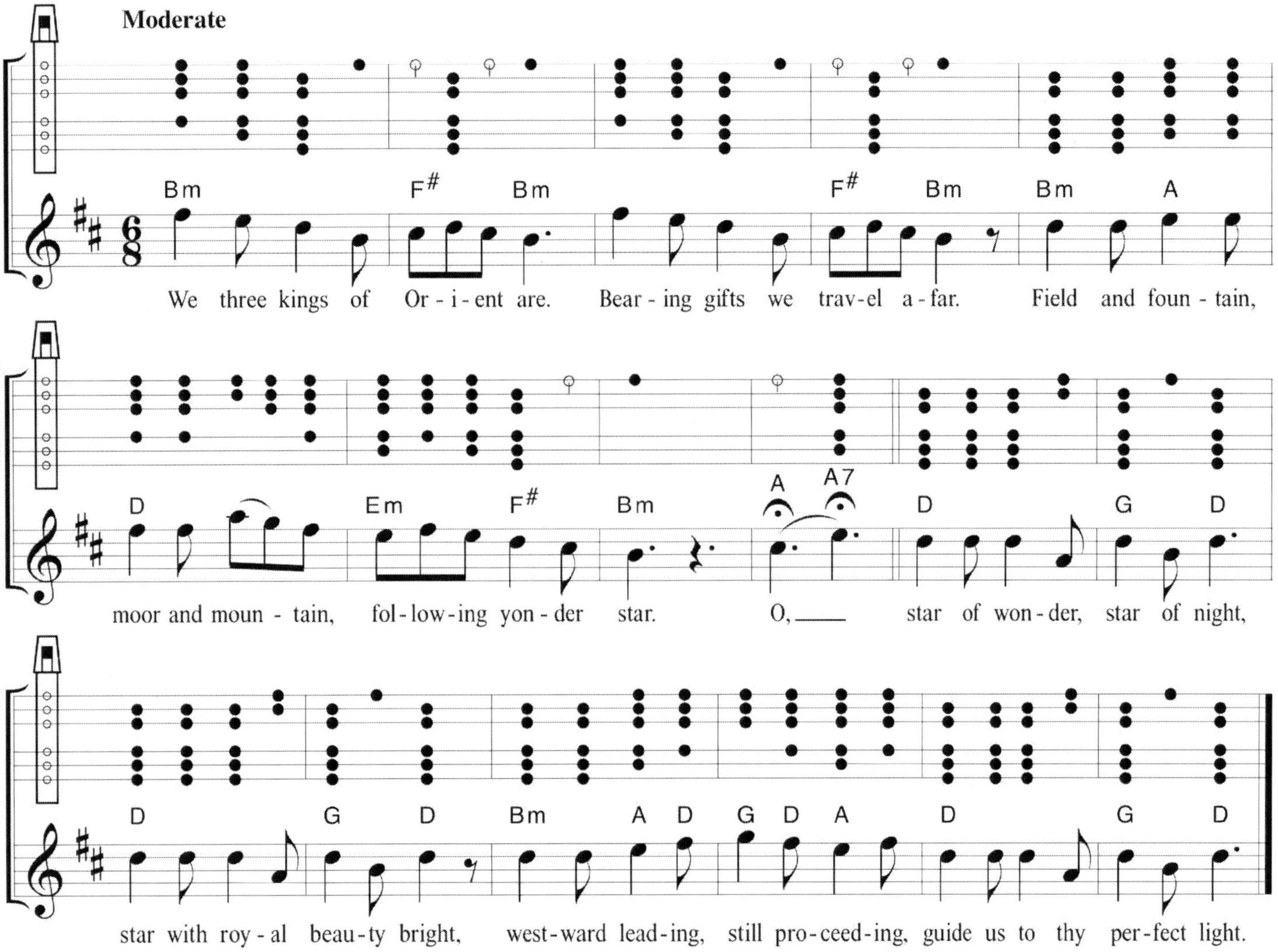

Moderate

Bm F# Bm F# Bm Bm A

We three kings of Or - i - ent are. Bear - ing gifts we trav-el a - far. Field and foun - tain,

D Em F# Bm A A7 D G D

moor and moun - tain, fol - low - ing yon - der star. O, ___ star of won - der, star of night,

D G D Bm A D G D A D G D

star with roy - al beau - ty bright, west - ward lead - ing, still pro - ceed - ing, guide us to thy per - fect light.

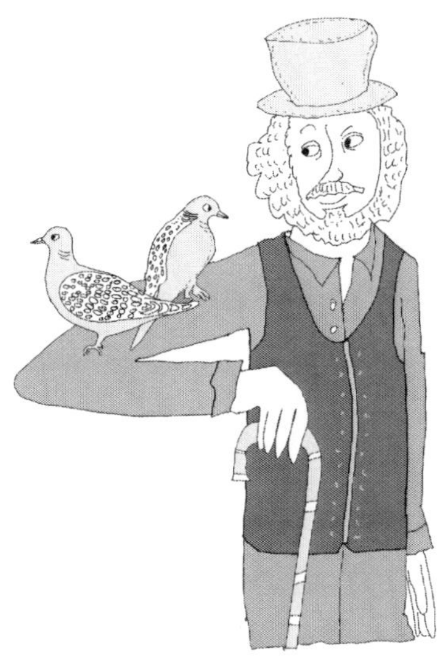

We Wish You a Merry Christmas

This is a traditional folk carol from the West Country of England. It was probably sung by wassailers who would request gifts as they went singing door to door. According to 19th century sources, the "figgy pudding" mentioned in the second verse would likely have been a raisin or plum pudding.

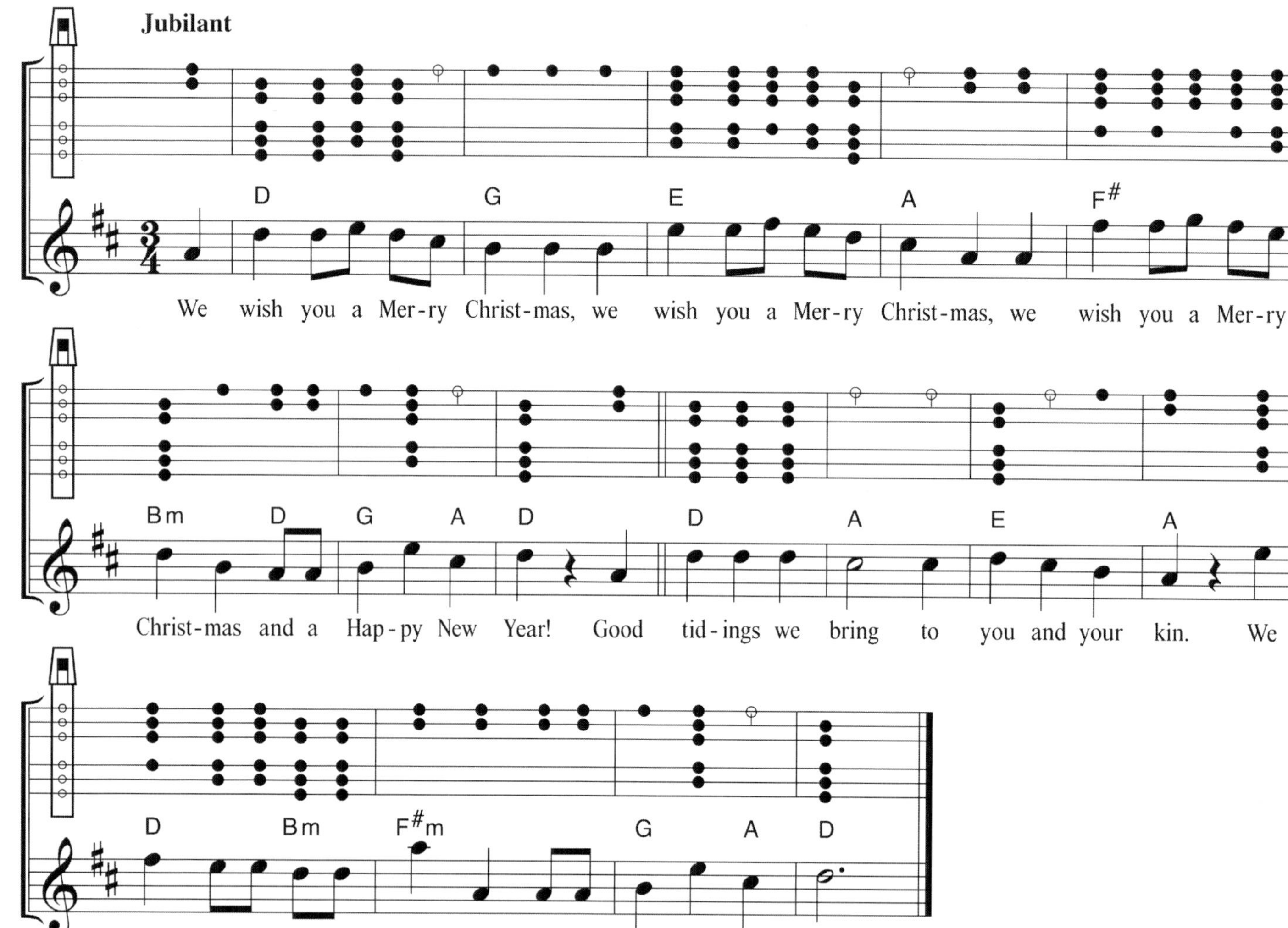

DUETS FOR TIN WHISTLES OR IRISH FLUTES

On the following six pages you'll find three duets. These can be played by tin whistles, flutes or other melodic instruments. You might also enjoy playing the harmony part while people are singing the song.

The melody parts appear on the left-facing pages. I have composed harmony parts, which are shown on the right-facing pages.

Audio recordings of these duets, in a number of different instrumental configurations, are available at www.melbay.com/30788MEB.

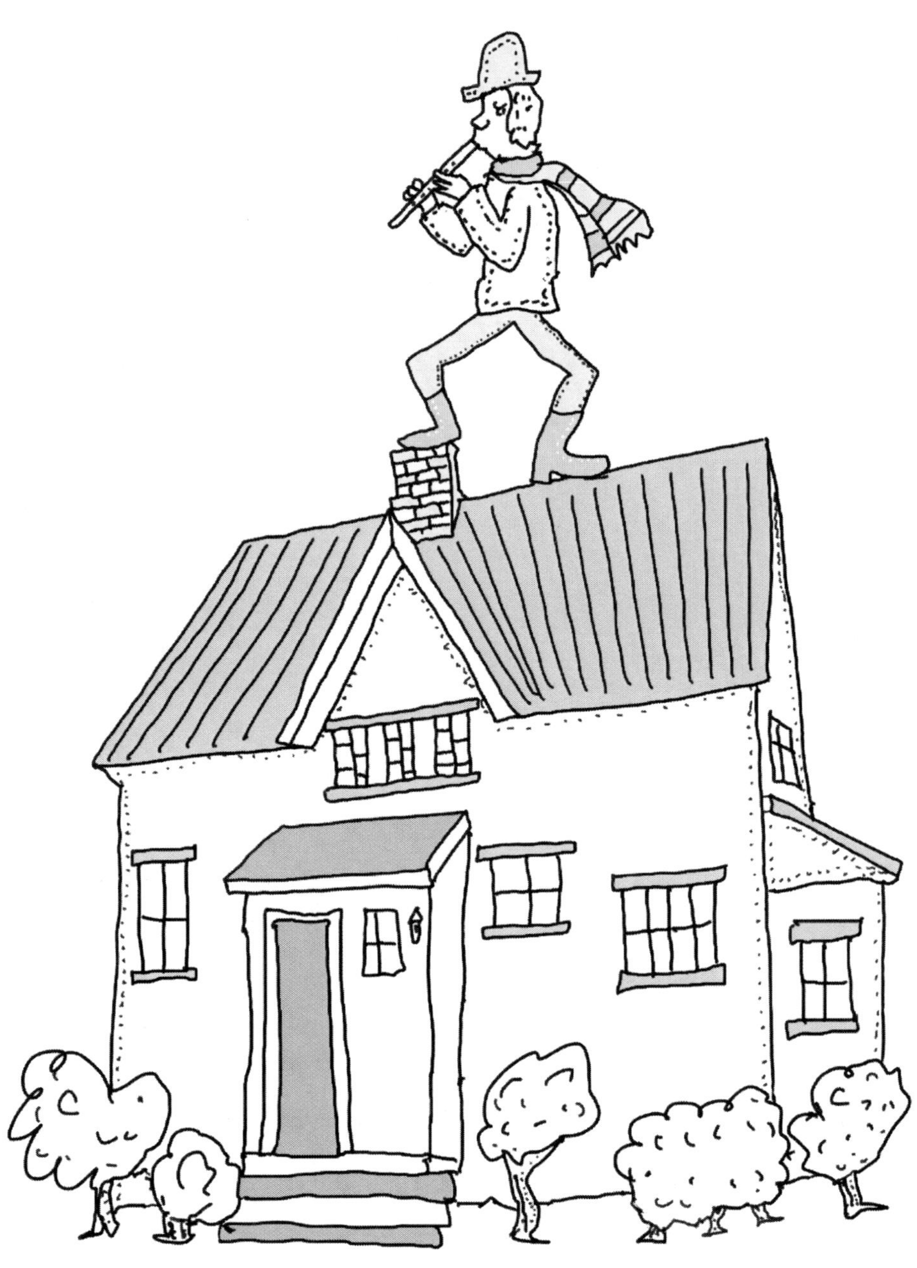

Ding Dong Merrily on High

Duet, Melody Part

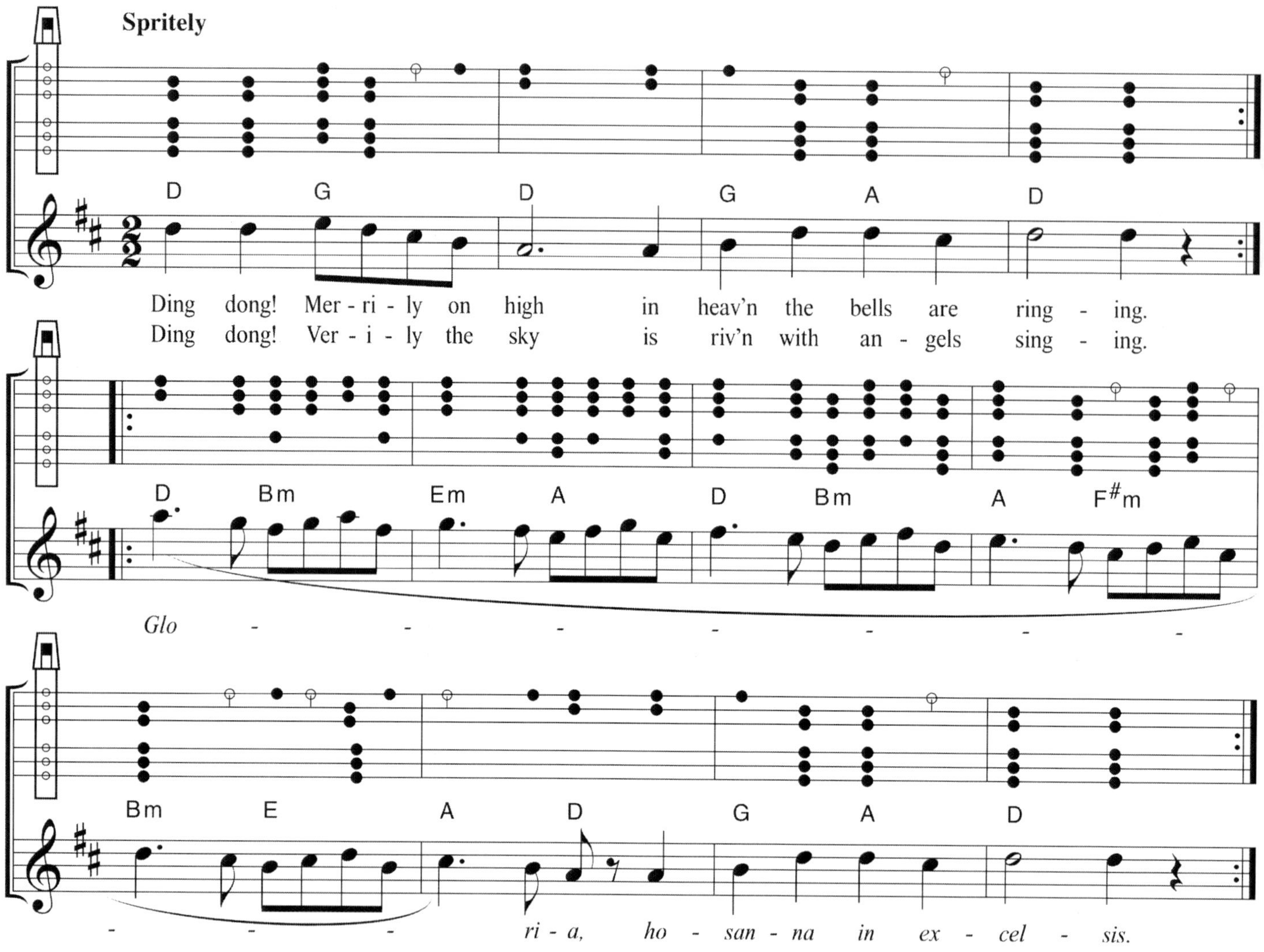

Spritely

D G D G A D

Ding dong! Mer - ri - ly on high in heav'n the bells are ring - ing.
Ding dong! Ver - i - ly the sky is riv'n with an - gels sing - ing.

D Bm Em A D Bm A F#m

Glo - - - - - - -

Bm E A D G A D

- - - ri - a, ho - san - na in ex - cel - sis.

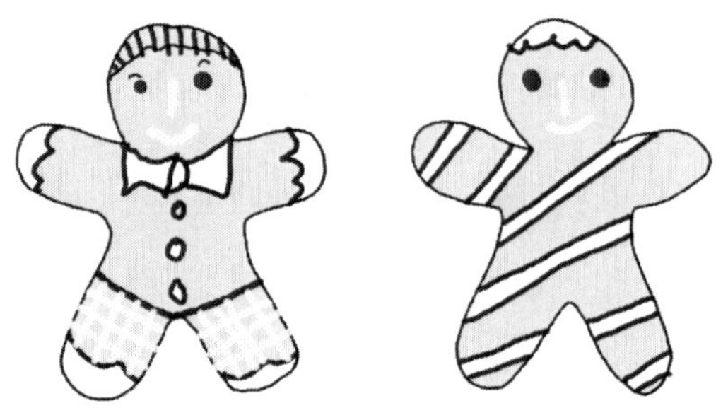

Ding Dong Merrily on High

Duet, Harmony Part

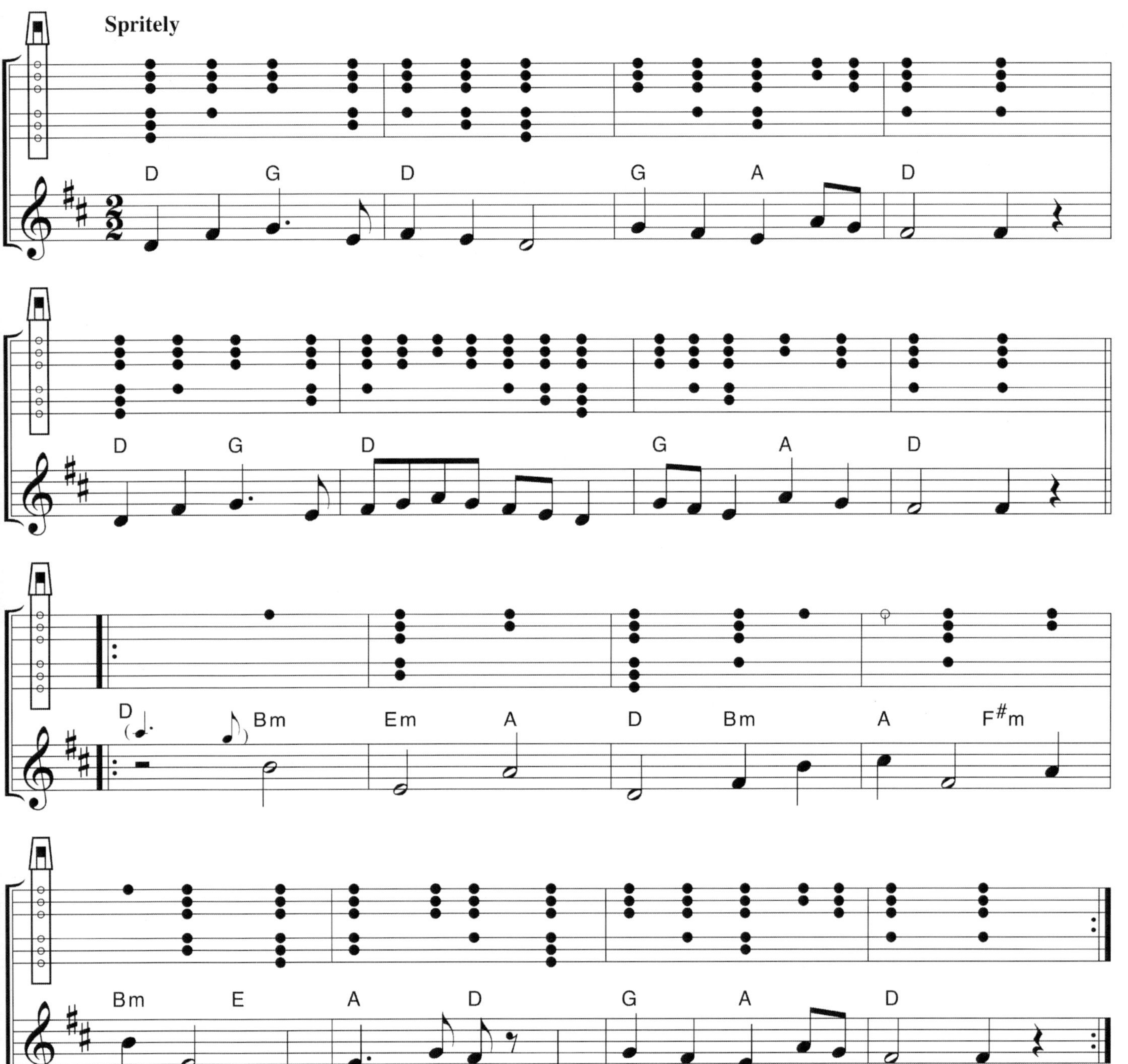

Silent Night
Duet, Melody Part

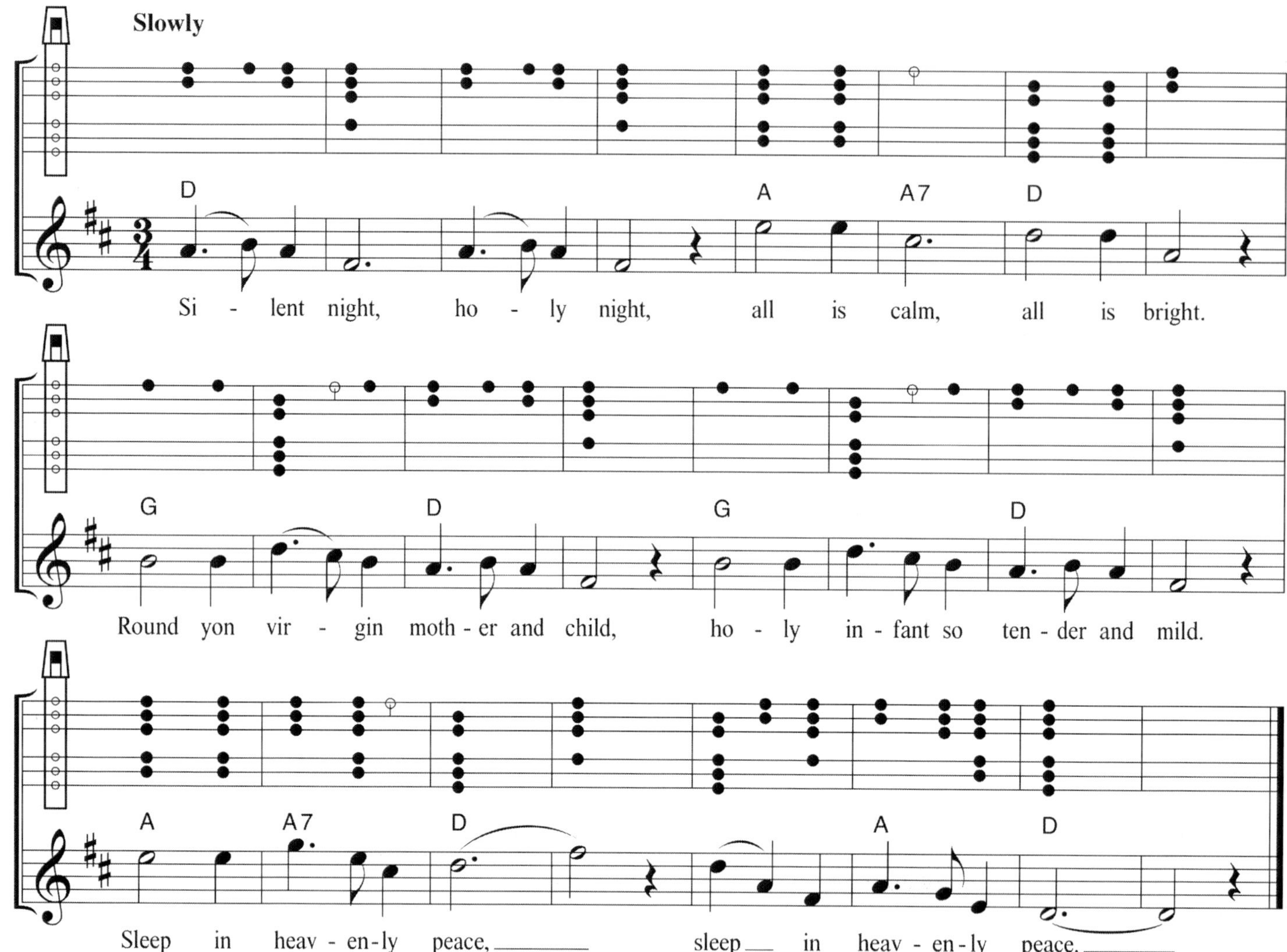

Silent Night

Duet, Harmony Part

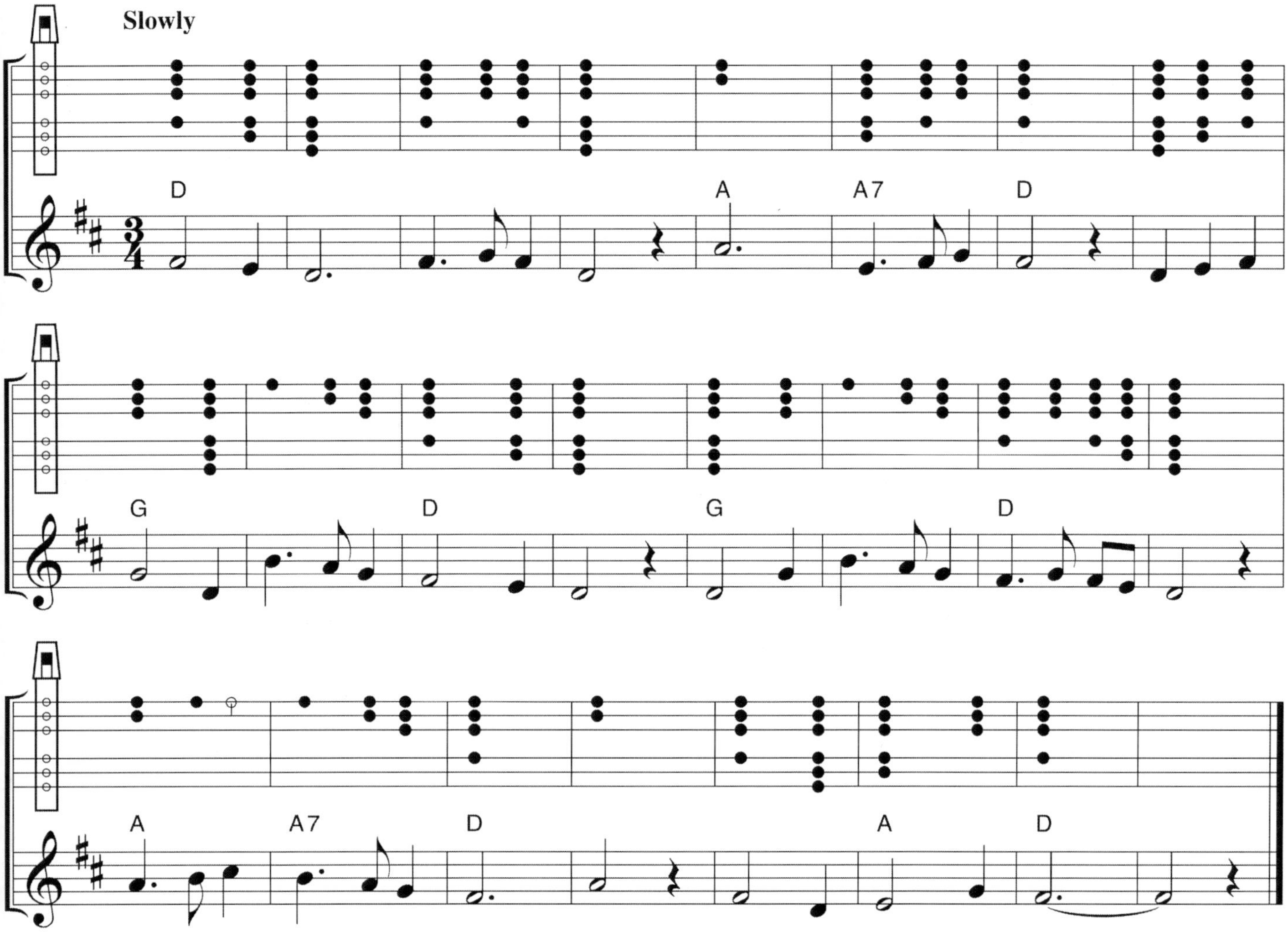

Slowly

D A A7 D

G D G D

A A7 D A D

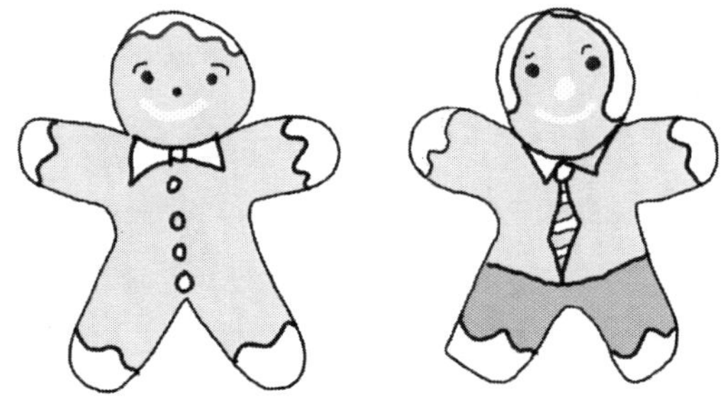

We Three Kings

Duet, Melody Part

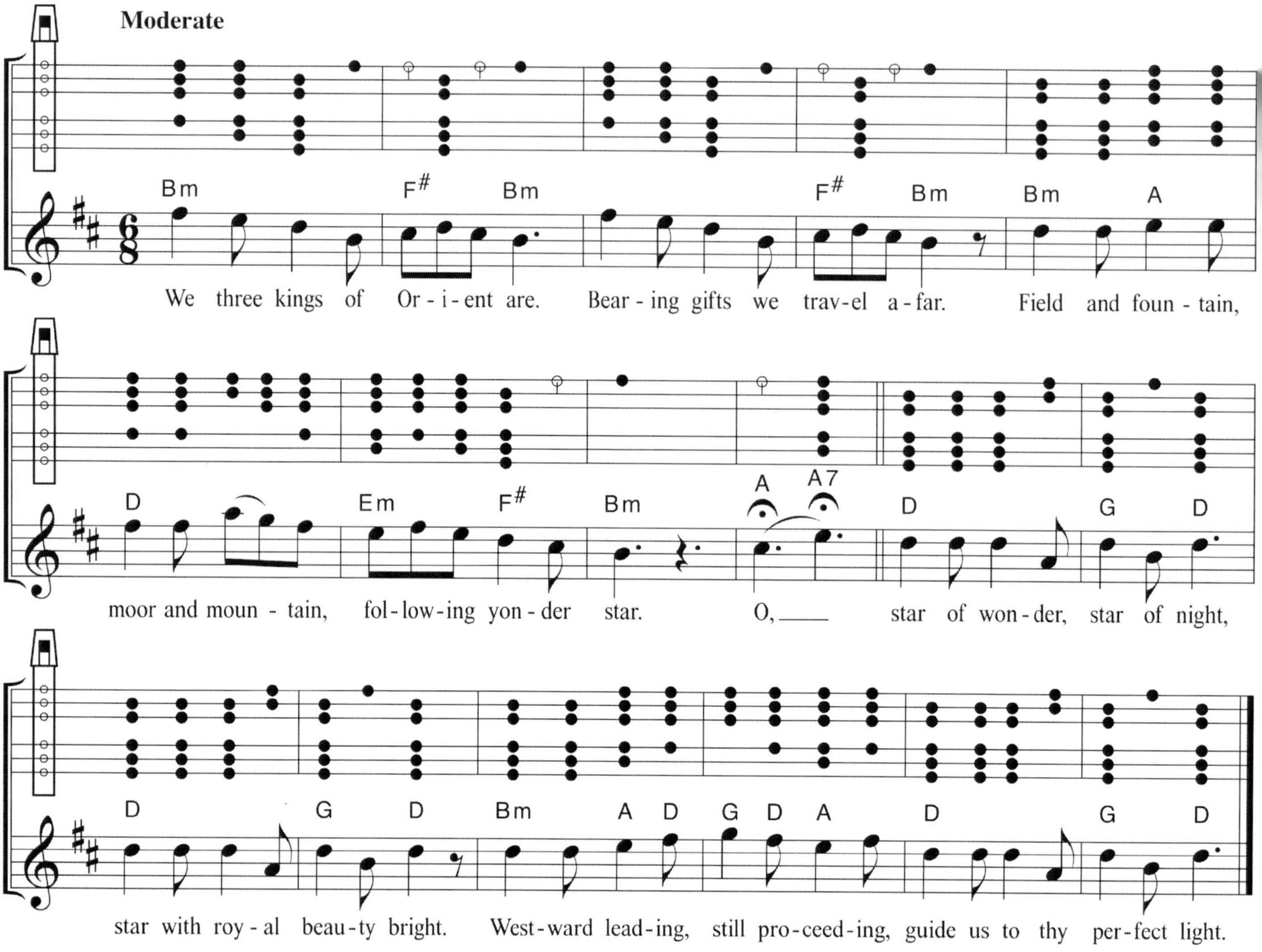

Moderate

Bm F# Bm F# Bm Bm A

We three kings of Or - i - ent are. Bear - ing gifts we trav - el a - far. Field and foun - tain,

D Em F# Bm A A7 D G D

moor and moun - tain, fol - low - ing yon - der star. O, star of won - der, star of night,

D G D Bm A D G D A D G D

star with roy - al beau - ty bright. West - ward lead - ing, still pro - ceed - ing, guide us to thy per - fect light.

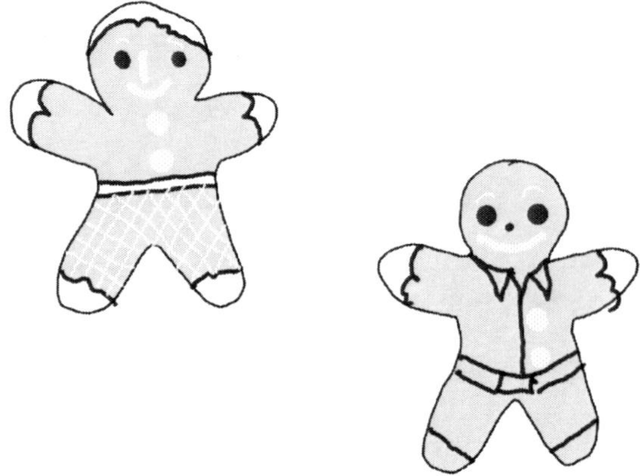

We Three Kings

Duet, Harmony Part

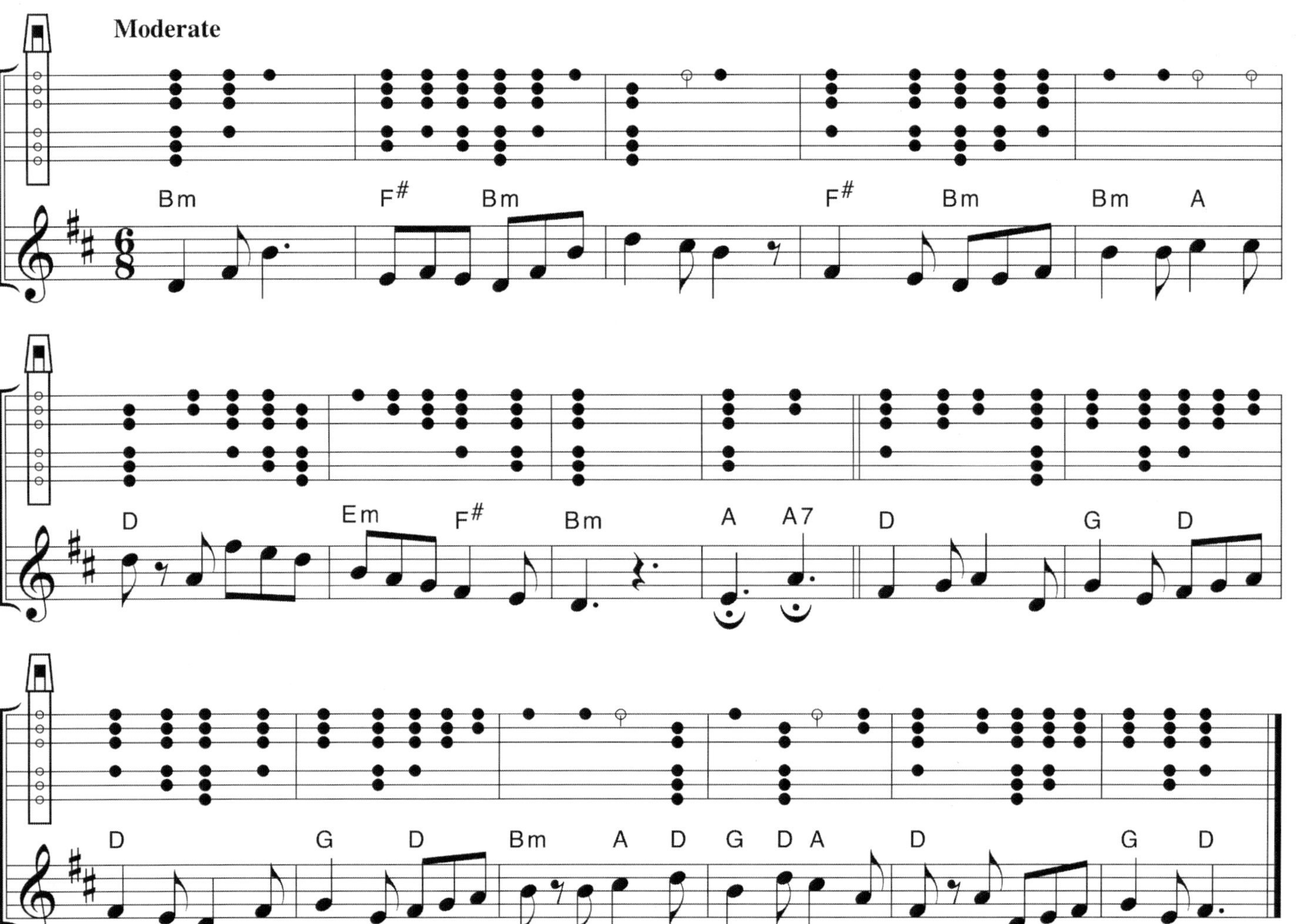

About the Author

Grey Larsen was born in 1955 in New York City. His family moved to Cincinnati, Ohio the following year. Beginning piano lessons at age four, he enjoyed a childhood and youth full of musical exploration, his inner world filled with the keyboard music of Bach and Mozart, as well as the early rock, R&B and Motown sounds on the radio, the songs of contemporary folk music interpreters and traditional Appalachian and Irish music. He started playing tin whistle at age 15. He plays Irish flute, tin whistle, anglo concertina, fiddle, piano, harmonium and guitar.

From 1970 to 1972 he studied at the Cincinnati College-Conservatory of Music before moving on, in 1973, to continue at the Oberlin Conservatory of Music in Oberlin, Ohio. While pursuing early music and composition on the one hand, he came ever more deeply under the spell of traditional music on the other, and for several years he followed these parallel streams with equal energy and dedication. In these and later years, he spent a great deal of time learning traditional Irish music from numerous elder Irish immigrants in Cincinnati and Cleveland, Ohio, most notably Co. Galway melodeon player Michael J. Kennedy (1900–1978), Co. Sligo flute player Tom Byrne (1920–2001) and Co. Leitrim fiddler Tom McCaffrey (1916–2006).

Upon completing a Bachelor of Music degree at Oberlin in 1976, the streams diverged. He bid a fond farewell to his academic path and set a course following his love of traditional music, exploring musical waterways that would branch, cross and rejoin over the decades.

Larsen leads a varied and rich musical life in Bloomington, Indiana and Camden, Maine as a performer, teacher, author, recording artist, recording and mastering engineer and music editor. Since the early 1970s he has also devoted himself to the traditional fiddle music of his native Midwest and Appalachia, in particular the music of southern Indiana fiddler Joe Dawson (1928–2012).

Also by Grey Larsen

Easy Tune Book for Tin Whistle or Irish Flute

Easy Favorites for Tin Whistle or Irish Flute

Other Books

The Essential Guide to Irish Flute and Tin Whistle
The Essential Tin Whistle Toolbox
First Lessons Tin Whistle
150 Gems of Irish Music for Tin Whistle
150 Gems of Irish Music for Flute
300 Gems of Irish Music for All Instruments
Down the Back Lane: Variation in Traditional Irish Dance Music

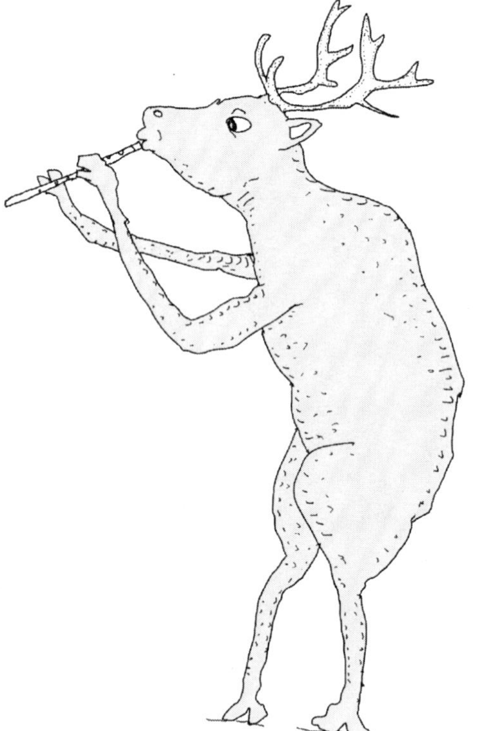

Recordings

With Cindy Kallet
- Cross the Water
- Welcome Day

With André Marchand
- The Orange Tree
- Les Marionnettes

With Paddy League
- The Green House
- Dark of the Moon

With Metamora
- Metamora
- The Great Road
- Morning Walk

With Malcolm Dalglish
- Banish Misfortune
- The First of Autumn
- Thunderhead

Solo
- The Gathering

Website

greylarsen.com

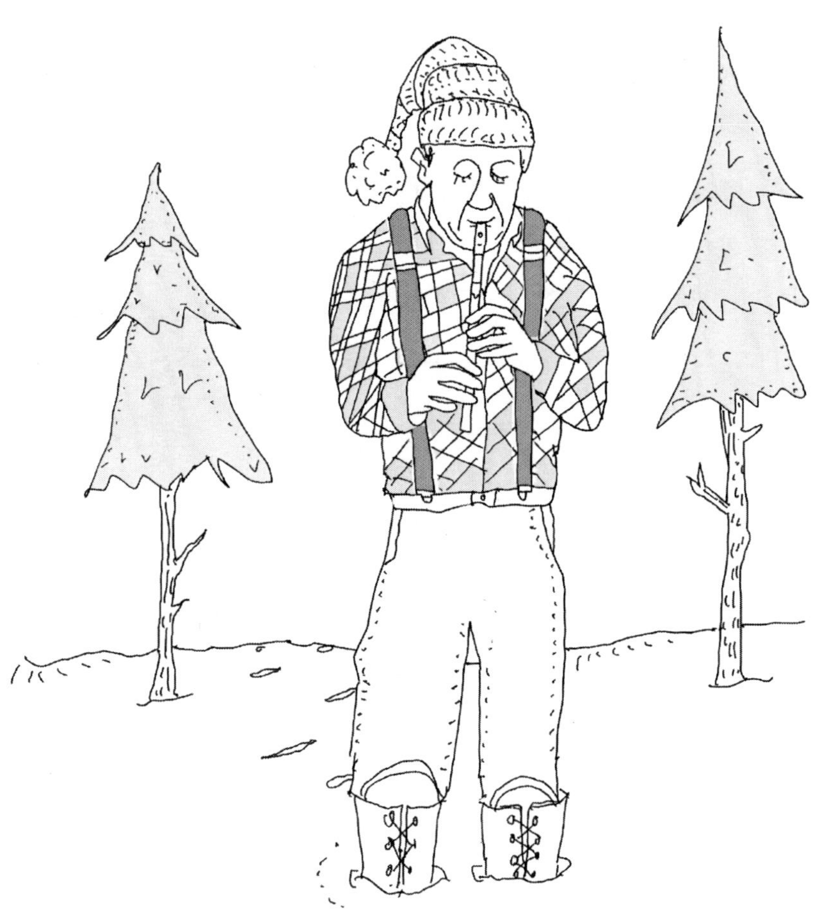

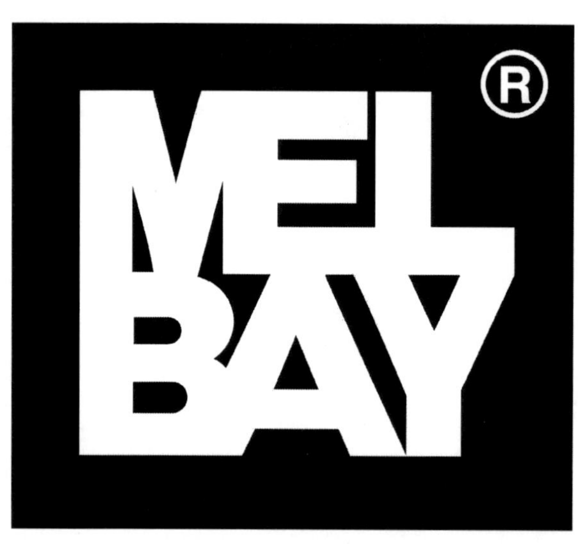

WWW.MELBAY.COM